Oct. 2000

Dearest Jim,

When I saw this book at the book fair I immediately thought of you! You were one of those few teachers who truly made a difference in the lives of many many students!

Hope you enjoy it!!

All my love!!
Linda

PRAISE FOR *Why I Teach*

"Teachers will laugh, cry, and gain inspiration all at once as they read these moving stories and remember why they joined the profession in the first place. The stories will also give teachers the courage to continue in their powerful mission of reaching and teaching children."

—ALAN M. BLANKSTEIN, founder of National Educational Service
and president of the HOPE* Foundation
(*Harnessing Optimism and Potential through Education)

"A must read for every teacher! After a good day at school, read one of these feel-good stories as a special treat. And on a bad day, these accounts of love and hope will re-inspire you to face tomorrow with a renewed belief in your ability to make a difference. As an added bonus, many of the stories contain great ideas for activities to do with your students to help them have confidence in themselves and in their ability to succeed."

—FRANK SICCONE, ED.D., author of *Educating the Heart* and
101 Ways to Develop Student Self-Esteem and Responsibility

"Stories of heart, stories of care, stories that make me proud that I belong to the teaching profession."

—MERRILL HARMIN, PH.D., author of
Strategies That Inspire Active Learning

"*Why I Teach* is uplifting, inspiring, and genuine. It demonstrates the truth about what real teaching is and what it must be: connecting with the whole human being."

—SANDI REDENBACH, M.ED.,
president of Esteem Seminar Programs

"Ms. Wright makes a major contribution to all educators by reminding us that our feelings are as important to the children we teach as our technical skills. These stories illustrate perfectly the humanity that all great teachers share."

—DR. RICHARD L. CURWIN,
co-author of *Discipline with Dignity*

Why I Teach

Inspirational True Stories
from Teachers Who
Make a Difference

ESTHER WRIGHT, M.A.

PRIMA PUBLISHING

This book is dedicated to my father, Hy Weiser who inspires me with his heart and wisdom and to Stephen Rosenblueth, my son, whom I love and appreciate beyond words.

PRIMA PUBLISHING and colophon are registered trademarks of Prima Communications, Inc.

All products mentioned in this book are trademarks of their respective companies.
Cover copy courtesy of Jane Bluestein, Ph.D., author of *Mentors, Masters, and Mrs. MacGregor*

Library of Congress Cataloging-in-Publication Data

Wright, Esther
Why I teach: inspirational true stories from teachers who make a difference/
[edited by] Esther Wright.
p. cm.
ISBN 0-7615-1099-0 (0-7615-2644-7 CUSTOM HARDCOVER)
1. Teachers—United States Anecdotes. 2. Teaching–United States Anecdotes. I. Wright, Esther.
LB1775.2.W49 1999
371.1—dc21   99-30814
CIP

00 01 02 03 04 05 AA 10 9 8 7 6 5 4 3 2
Printed in the United States of America

HOW TO ORDER
Single copies may be ordered from Prima Publishing, P.O. Box 1260BK, Rocklin, CA 95677; telephone (916) 632-4400. Quantity discounts are also available. On your letterhead, include information concerning the intended use of the books and the number of books you wish to purchase.

Visit us online at www.primalifestyles.com

Contents

CONTENTS

Foreword

IF YOU HAD asked me back in the beginning, to tell you why I teach, I don't know how I might have answered. It wasn't the money—back in my days as a teaching intern, I was bringing home a mere $318 a month, which wasn't much even then. It wasn't the hours—between graduate school and losing the battle to stay one step ahead of my thirty-nine fifth graders, I was putting in ridiculously long days. And it certainly wasn't the chance to exercise my genius as an instructor—I was lucky if I could get through one day without a fist fight breaking out.

No, there wasn't much glory in working with kids who greeted me with, "I don't *do* reading," before I'd had a chance to learn their names. Nor was it heartwarming to teach kids who saw me more as an annoyance than an inspiration, kids who couldn't care less that all I'd ever wanted my entire life was to be a teacher.

I cried a lot my first year. I cried the day my whole class failed what *I* thought was a simple pre-test. I cried the day my kids wouldn't sit down and be quiet while my supervisor was in the room. I cried the day a parent said that maybe her son would do better with an "older" teacher. And I cried the day I visited the home of one of my most difficult students and found her mother falling-down drunk before lunchtime.

So what kept me in the game, especially that first year? Looking back, it took remarkably little to renew my sense of hope, or at least suggest that maybe all was not lost. I would come *this close* to throwing in the towel when a child would uncharacteristically come to class prepared, make a positive behavioral change, or help a classmate. I'd be sure I couldn't make it through the day when someone would suddenly *get* subtraction or appear excited about a subject we were about to discuss. And just as I was about to give up, they'd finally sit still for a story or laugh at one of my jokes.

For other teachers, perhaps it's the progress, imperceptible as it may seem at times, the little connections, a hug here and there, or the realization that we might well be the only source of encouragement some child is getting right now. Perhaps deep down there's the possibility that our excitement, or even our good intentions, somehow makes a dent, that our caring and commitment allow us, inevitably, to touch the future. But we give what we give because we can't *not* give, and we give in the best of faith, because the evidence of our devotion is sometimes long in coming. We are tested again and again, and sometimes we just keep coming back for no good reason besides the fact that, for better or worse, we are called to teach. Maybe this is something only another teacher can understand: It's not just what we do. It's who we are.

JANE BLUESTEIN, PH.D.
Albuquerque, New Mexico

Acknowledgments

THIS BOOK WAS a labor of love that could not have been completed without the participation and support of many people. First, I wish to thank Prima Publishing for offering me the privilege and opportunity to put this book together. Special thanks to Jamie Miller and Karen Naungayan for their editing input and assistance.

I am very grateful to the hundreds of dedicated teachers who opened their hearts and shared their inspirational stories with me. I wish I could have used more of the wonderful vignettes I received. Perhaps there will be an opportunity in a future volume.

Special friends unselfishly offered their time and energy to the project. I am most grateful to Ron Dumas, the wonderful man in my life, who spent countless hours patiently sharing his technical skills and knowledge. I never would have completed the manuscript in a timely manner without Ron's support. He read, scanned, and formatted many of the stories. He coached and supervised the process, often in the wee hours of the morning, making sure the manuscript was just right.

Many thanks to my dear friend Sandi Redenbach, a "teacher of the heart," who generously assisted with reviewing and selecting stories. Her feedback was invaluable. Thanks also to Barbara Reider, a recently retired, exemplary teacher, who also volunteered her time to read and edit. Hugs to my friend and colleague, Dianne Maxon, who supported me in the process of gathering and reviewing stories and is always there for me when I need her.

Over the years, I have been blessed with great coaching and caring from my friend and mentor, Dr. Frank Siccone, who continues to be an inspiration. And finally, my deepest appreciation to the staff and volunteers affiliated with Landmark Education Corporation. These wonderful people have supported my commitment to life-long learning, and have helped sustain my love and passion for teaching throughout my career.

Introduction

AS PEOPLE READ this collection of stories, one thing will become abundantly clear: Teachers are extraordinary people with a passionate commitment to make a difference in the lives of others.

The process of compiling these stories was a very profound and inspirational one for me. Not only did I have the pleasure of making new friends in the world of education; I also had the opportunity to spend many hours reliving my experiences as a classroom teacher in San Francisco's public schools.

During the past year while gathering stories, I would visit my local post office to retrieve teacher submissions, then walk to a local cafe for lunch, where I would read the treasures that appeared in my post office box. On more than one occasion, diners seated at nearby tables stared and wondered why this middle-aged woman sobbed while munching on her sandwich. Tears streamed down my face as I read the powerful words of teachers who gave their blood, sweat, and tears to a child (or a whole classroom of children), and produced miracles that made a tremendous difference in the lives of students. It is evident in many of the stories that countless children will now have happy, productive futures because they were blessed with gifted and dedicated teachers.

I have always considered teaching to be the most honorable of all professions. The stories in this book confirm that notion. I am reminded that it takes heart and wisdom to be a master teacher and there is much to learn from students, in fact, they are often *our* greatest teachers.

If you are called to be a teacher, consider it a sacred trust. For you, these stories will illustrate that with your chosen profession comes a never ending process of learning and growing. If you are parent, child, sibling, spouse, or friend of a teacher, you will discover a new and profound respect for the challenges that teachers face in their day-to-day work. If you are a young person thinking about becoming a teacher, you will learn many important lessons about what it really takes to impact the lives of children. Perhaps the most important lesson I have learned is that it takes more than a lesson plan or curriculum to teach a child. Teaching requires large doses of patience, compassion, and love.

I look forward to sharing these stories with you. I hope they will touch your heart and warm your soul. I hope they will serve as an acknowledgment to teachers and students everywhere.

A Teaching Legacy

I REMEMBER THE first time I confronted the question, "Why does one teach?" I had just overcome a very difficult and chaotic period of my life after getting my B.A. and M.A. degrees in Vocal Performance. Not only was it tough getting through school while supporting myself, but I was attending San Francisco State University during the turmoil and unrest of the 1960s. I felt drained and had no idea what the future held. All I could think of was finishing my final recital and moving beyond the struggle I had faced those many years while going to school.

At one time I dreamed of becoming an opera singer or actress, but on the day of my final recital, one of my professors stopped me in the hall and told me that a local school district was desperately seeking music teachers. Up to that point, I had resisted joining my parents' profession, in spite of my father's belief that I was born to be a teacher. In that moment, however, I considered that maybe this was divine intervention.

The following day I called the school district and set up an interview. I was hired on the spot! My head spun with excitement.

The next few months were spent learning my job, traveling between three schools, writing lesson plans, and staying healthy. Gradually, the unconditional love of my students began to seep into my soul and heal the unhappy and demoralizing experience of my own schooling. I realized these beautiful children of every color and hue could see and understand my inherent goodness. Unlike the way my teachers had viewed me, these children looked beyond the surface and saw my loving heart. My students thought I was beautiful and the best music teacher in the world! They met my car in the morning and followed me around like the pied piper! It was almost a bit frightening. They believed in me and followed my lead in whatever instructions I gave them. This was heady stuff for a young teacher.

On my first visit home that year, I had a long conversation with my father about teaching. By then, he had been teaching for thirty-five years and was working as a junior-college professor. I told him I was a bit overwhelmed to have so much trust and devotion from my students. His reply was one I shall never forget. He said, "Good! You *should* feel in awe of your power. It is a sacred trust that you must never violate. You must never believe that you are as great as they think you are. You are simply a vessel through which your love of music and your love of children will develop these youngsters into responsible and loving beings."

At that moment I understood why my Dad was such a great teacher. I had always taken for granted his loving support while singing in choirs he conducted. It was during our conversation, however, that I began to understand the true nature of the gift of teaching. Perhaps we are keepers of the souls of our students, even though they may not know it. We may never know what our influence has been, but we must be the beacon of light towards their rich and full futures.

> *Perhaps we are keepers of the souls of our students, even though they may not know it.*

Looking back over the years, I realize that I have taught at every level and in many different venues, from private to public schools, teaching rich and poor students alike. Yet, I always come back to my father's sound advice and realize *it is not about me.* I am only a vessel for the Creator's love to imbue the student with the knowledge that they are capable, precious human beings who can and will make their mark in the world.

VILETTA SKILLMAN
Redlands, California

3

A Very Special Delivery

*W*HILE SIXTH PERIOD charges toward their lockers, I glance across Room 815. Content, I recall the earlier scene of twenty-seven sixth graders actively engaged in the writing and analysis of poetry. I relish their developing maturity and serious commentary. My mind drifts back to the day's activities, and silently I rejoice for one of my fifth-period students. The honesty with which he shared his struggle to stay out of trouble and remain in school impressed me. I was pleased.

Almost effortlessly, I organize papers and folders, quickly preparing for an afternoon of meetings. I am unaware of the young man standing in the doorway, waiting for my attention. "Are you Ms. Moller?" he inquires. "Yes," I respond, anticipating a message from a colleague. "Here." He hands me a manila folder and walks off. Stapled to the front of the folder is a computer-generated cover with the words, "It's a special delivery for Ms. Moller." Interested, I open the folder. Inside, a forest-green piece of construction paper, folded toward the center from the left and right sides, prominently displays a large red heart. In block letters, written on each corner, are the words "Thank you." A small note in the bottom left hand corner reads, "from Andrew." I shed a tear while opening the card, emotionally preparing to read.

Dear Ms. Moller,

Thank you for helping me when I needed it. Thank you for staying after school to help me with my homework and projects. Because of you, I will go to high school. Thank you for everything you did for me. Thank you for getting me through middle school. One more thing: You are the best teacher!

Sincerely,
Andrew

Overcome, I sit and think of Andrew. Yes, you are going to high school, I say to myself. And for that, *I* want to thank *you.*

I WAS A first-year teacher when Andrew and I met. Frankly, we had little interaction during that fourth-period English class. It always frustrated me when he did not return homework or come to class prepared. He began most in-class assignments, but rarely completed or turned them in. I commented on his disorganized binder and lectured him about the importance of homework and living up to one's potential. I varied activities, hoping to give him ways to be more successful. Still, Andrew was reluctant to participate and made little progress.

One afternoon, in November of that year, Andrew stood silently behind me. In a quiet yet stern way he said, "I need help with reading. I don't understand." My heart sank, for at that very moment, I felt like a failure. How could I have not known?

Formally, I was Andrew's mentor. Informally, he was mine.

I suggested that Andrew and I meet during lunch. Although he was reluctant to lose time with his friends, he agreed. Almost daily Andrew would return to the sixth-grade hallway balancing a lunch tray atop of his discombobulated binder. Together we created agendas to structure his time. We organized his binder, read together, completed work, and got to know each other. I was impressed with his determination and drive. I was intrigued that each small accomplishment delighted him. Formally, I was Andrew's mentor. Informally, he was mine.

Andrew taught me how to teach. He taught me how to be patient, consistent, and caring. He taught me that there are many ways to be intelligent. Andrew is why I teach.

ON THE DAY I receive my special delivery, I reflect upon the road we had traveled. Following sixth grade, Andrew and I continued to meet on an academic and personal level. Through ice cream and Yahtzee, work and play, we grew. Now he was ready for more. Eighth-grade graduation would be in three months and indeed, Andrew would be going to high school. The sheer thought of Andrew navigating through the masses of that large building frightened me. Yet, I knew it was time.

Dear Andrew,

Thank you for all that you have given me. You were there to let me help you. Thank you for teaching me how to be a better teacher. If I was "the best teacher" it was only because you were my student. I will forever be proud of what you have achieved.

Fondly,
Ms. Moller

PAULINE MOLLER
Bethesda, Maryland

Love and Loss

I HAD BEEN teaching about five years when I became pregnant with my first child. I carried the baby for about four-and-a-half months and then heartbreakingly had a miscarriage. I was very upset by the incident and stayed home from work for two days to regain my composure. I had already told the students in my first-grade class that I was going to have a baby, so I dreaded going back to school and facing the children with the sad news. I had no idea how to explain what had happened and was afraid I would burst into tears should any of the children ask about the baby.

When I returned to school, the teacher across the hall from my classroom took me aside and hugged me. She explained that she had already informed my class of the loss and that she had asked them not to mention it to me. I was very grateful to her. I walked into my classroom and began teaching. The students never mentioned the baby or the loss. I was truly inspired by how sensitive and kind these first graders handled this unfortunate event.

Several months passed and gradually my pain eased. One afternoon while taking the children to the restroom, one of my darling boys came up to me. He looked into my eyes and asked me to lean closer. When I was very close, he whispered, "I know what it's like to be lost. I got lost once, too. Did you check the grocery store really good before you left?" His words brought a smile to my face. I assured him that I had searched every possible place and that my baby had gone somewhere much better.

Over the years when I think of my miscarriage, I no longer feel an overwhelming sense of sadness. I am grateful that this sweet young man, in his infinite caring and wisdom, made me laugh in the face of a very painful loss.

LISA DEGNAN
Irmo, South Carolina

Learning the Ropes

*T*HERE IS A moment when the struggle to master an activity or subject ceases and the action becomes familiar and regimented. Teaching is a strand of these moments, strung together to create a career.

Collin was one of the most driven and courageous young boys I'd ever worked with. He had a great sense of humor, an ability to manipulate large numbers and operations in his head, the drive and skill of an athlete, a talent for writing poetry, the love of his friends, and a sense of justice that would make Martin Luther King Jr. proud. Despite all this, he faced challenges like every one of us. Learning to read short vowels and forming his lower case letters took great work and practice for him. But unlike most of us, Collin was born without his left hand and wrist.

He adapted to a world of two-handedness quite well. He swung a mean bat and was driven at the age of three to be the best T-ball player on the block.

Collin and I met years before I was ever his teacher. I got to know him while baby-sitting for his parents. I challenged him to build a ramp for a tennis ball with his blocks. This activity was very important to Collin. A few years later when he walked into my first-grade classroom, he was excited to have a teacher who would challenge him.

Collin's parents and I met regularly to talk about the adaptations and special needs that he would have around the classroom and in the gym. Collin needed some modifications to his recorder in music, a card holder for math games, a strap for holding a floor hockey stick with his arm, and the flexibility in P.E. to dribble or catch. In first grade, Collin chose not to use a prosthetic hand and wrist. He was able to do most activities that his two-handed peers could do and he prided himself on his athletic abilities.

I attempted to anticipate and lay ground for upcoming events in the classroom and P.E., but occasionally it was trial by fire for Collin. There was one gym activity that created tremendous anxiety for Collin and me: rope climbing. Collin and I had honest conversations about the physical challenges he faced. He was worried that he wasn't going to be able to climb the ropes: "I couldn't last year and everyone else could."

I was worried for him, too. The gym was the center of the school, and the forty-foot ropes that hung from the ceiling appeared to require two legs, two feet, and two hands to ascend. Because Collin was well-known throughout the school for his ability to play baseball and basketball, he was faced with a "public" challenge of upholding his reputation as an athlete.

Collin and I developed a plan. For weeks he worked on exercises that would strengthen his upper body: chin-ups, ball bouncing, push-ups against a wall. When he felt confident about his strength, he and I took time in the gym to begin to hang and swing on the ropes. I corralled some teachers to patrol the curious onlookers that peered in the windows of the gym doors, allowing him the privacy to concentrate. Collin let me assist him in getting onto the rope. He'd sit on the knot and swing as we talked about the muscles he would use to pull himself up. Over time, he taught himself to get up, hold on, and swing on the rope. This alone felt like a major success to Collin, since in kindergarten he had needed to be lifted on to the rope. But getting up by himself wasn't enough for him. "This," he stated, "isn't *climbing* the ropes." He was absolutely determined to master this skill!

The day finally came when the whole P.E. class was asked to practice climbing the ropes. Collin and I had planned the day so he would have time to prepare. As the class got started, the instructions for the various stations were given. The children cheered happily, "We finally get to do the ropes!" Soon there were children swinging from each of the four ropes. For some of the kids, just getting on and struggling up two or three feet was a big accomplishment. For other children, rope climbing was quite easy. These climbers shimmied right up to the top, touched the top knot, shouted to friends across the gym for praise, and proceeded to slide down.

By then the energy in the gym was buzzing. Several children had experienced great success and hopped up and down with joy; others flopped on the big blue mats huffing and puffing from the difficulty of the climb. The whistle blew for the last group to take its turn on the ropes. Collin bounded over to the mats, removed his sneakers, and got himself onto the knot. The other children in the group were really impressed and shared their memories of Collin sitting in the chair last year not wanting to climb at all. Collin, recognized for his hard work, beamed with delight. "You can't cheer yet.... Watch!" Collin shouted. He pulled himself up four inches with his right hand, then pressed the rope between his left arm and his torso. He repositioned his right hand and pulled himself up another four inches, holding on with his left arm and torso. By now the whole class was gathered around the mats, chanting, "Collin! Collin! Collin!" Collin held on, looked around at his audience of friends and in amazement marveled, "I climbed the rope! I climbed the rope!"

THERE IS A moment when the struggle to master an activity ceases and the action becomes familiar and regimented. Teaching is a strand of these moments, strung together to create a career. Collin taught me to wait just that extra moment, until the struggle becomes mastery. That is why I teach.

MARIANNE O'GRADY
Mill Valley, California

The Mechanics of Learning

*T*HE YEAR THAT Sonny walked into my second-grade classroom on the first day of school sporting that broad toothy trademark smile turned out to be one of the most memorable of my career. Sonny was big for his age with a handsome face, a flair for art, and a reputation that preceded him. His interests in school remained within the boundaries of lunch and recess, and requiring him to focus on any element of academics was a major challenge. In short, Sonny was a management problem.

We struggled through the first two months of school with little success. "Miz Ferris, I forgot my homework," or "Miz Ferris, I didn't get time to do this," Sonny would drawl offering his all-too-frequent excuses. Sonny spent his time finding interesting things to rattle inside his desk when he was in his seat. When he wasn't, which was most of the time, he made his daily rounds of the classroom collecting stray items in the learning centers, checking out available opportunities for diversion, and trying to recruit others to join him in his quests.

I had tried every strategy that I could think of to hold Sonny's attention to academic tasks, but so far nothing had worked. Then came a day of discovery and an idea that would turn the tide! It was just before Thanksgiving, and we were on the bus headed to the high school auditorium to see a live performance of a children's classic by a professional troupe of actors. Most of the students were chattering away about the play and the background knowledge they had, but Sonny was working on a loose flap of vinyl hanging on the side of the seat. Then we passed a construction site, and Sonny came out of his seat pointing and yelling, "Look! There's a backhoe! And it's just like my uncle's—the one I run. Look, Miz Ferris!"

I knew about Sonny's fascination with backhoes because even though we only had show-and-tell once a month, he had brought his bright yellow Tonka toy backhoe many times. Each time he brought it, he "smuggled" it out during recess to dig in the dirt. The yard-duty teacher always turned a blind eye in his direction, satisfied that Sonny was actively engaged in peaceful play.

The day of the performance, Sonny's attention to the play was minimal because the actors wore costumes instead of hard hats and danced around the stage instead of pulling levers on backhoes. My attention to the play was also fragmented because my mind kept jumping to the possibility of involving Sonny in mini-lessons with backhoes. Would it work? Could I reach him that way? I wasn't sure, but it was worth a try.

That night I set out to design a backhoe curriculum for Sonny. Fortunately, my husband owned and operated a heavy equipment company and received catalogs in the mail almost daily. I enlisted his help. He located backhoe pictures while I cut and sorted them, all the while picking his brain for basic information that I could translate into second-grade vocabulary.

The next morning I presented Sonny his backhoe project along with his somewhat modified regular work in language arts. His face lit up when he saw the picture of the bright yellow backhoe. Together we worked on the reading passage, and then I watched him tackle the sentence section with an enthusiasm that I had seen only at lunch and on the playground. When he finished his project, which was a first, I didn't have to ask him to turn it in. He was waving it in front of my face with that big grin radiating like a lantern. Did I dare ask myself if I had found the key to succeeding with Sonny?

I continued Sonny's lessons using backhoes. After several days I discovered that Sonny had kept these projects in his desk, and another idea hit me. Why not collect them and bind them into a book? Sonny was thrilled by the thought. He spent hours designing his book cover and making his title page, learning about title page parts, capital letters, and other skills in incidental ways. This was the first of three books that Sonny would bind and publish that year. Sometimes Sonny would dictate ideas to me, and other times he would write backhoe information or experiences on his own. One morning he showed me a detailed backhoe drawing and said, "Miz Ferris, my uncle helped me with this last night. When I couldn't get the hydraulic part right, I called him and he came over and showed me how it fit together." I was amazed that Sonny had taken that initiative for learning and further astonished and thrilled that his uncle had become involved.

One day my husband stopped in at an equipment place where he saw one of their company baseball caps. The cap had a yellow backhoe on the front, so he got one for my ongoing project with Sonny. I placed the cap on the bookshelf next to my desk the next morning. Sonny came bounding in with his usual energy and scanned the room for any interesting opportunity for action. When he saw the cap, he stopped dead in his tracks. He looked at me, then looked at the cap. I saw some degree of realization began to trickle into his mind as that familiar grin slowly spread across his face. I still did not say a word. He watched me with suspicion for a while, and then I asked, "Sonny, what do you think about that cap?"

"I like it," he answered.

"Would you like to have it?" I continued. Sonny nodded his head, but with an expression that clearly signaled his concern about any kind of bargain that was behind this deal. I quietly explained that if he worked hard and followed the classroom rules for the next three days, he could have the cap. I knew that three days for Sonny would require just about all the effort he could summon, but I also believed he was up to the challenge.

The entire class seemed to make Sonny *their* project for the next three days! It was as though he had his own special cheering section monitoring his every move and willing him to reach his goal. And what a goal it was! At the end of that third day, I happily presented Sonny his "gold medal"—a seemingly insignificant baseball cap with a yellow backhoe embroidered on the front, a cap that stood as a landmark in Sonny's learning. In addition to the cap, Sonny had also earned the support and approval of his classmates, another first in his young life. He also earned a degree of confidence and pride that comes with effort and perseverance in doing a job well.

News of Sonny's accomplishments spread, and suddenly everyone wanted a part in his project. Administrators, school-board members, and other visitors would often stop by to hear Sonny read from one of his three published backhoe books and to admire his artwork and his handwriting. He truly basked in the glow of his new-found fame.

In the spring we studied transportation in social studies. One of the culminating projects was a three-dimensional mural that the students were required to design and construct. During our planning and brainstorming session, Jonathan, one of the class leaders, suggested, "Mrs. Ferris, we should let Sonny be the project chairman because he knows so much about vehicles, and he's so good in art." Jonathan's suggestion was met with enthusiastic nods of approval. To this day, I still hold in my memory the image of Sonny witnessing his nomination. He beamed, ready to explode with joy. I believe he finally understood and appreciated the value of peer acceptance.

Sonny continued to struggle with academics, but we had crossed a big hurdle and found a way for him to experience some success that year. Unfortunately, he entered third grade in much the same way as he had entered second: unmotivated, off-task, and showing minimum performance. At the end of the first week of school, his third-grade teacher stopped me in the hall. She wanted some advice about helping Sonny. By coincidence, Sonny walked down the hall as we were talking. I asked him if he still had his three bound books from second grade. "Oh, yes ma'am. I do! I've got 'em right here," he answered.

"Right here?" I asked, thinking he had misunderstood my question.

"Yes, ma'am. Right here at school in my desk."

Sure enough, Sonny had brought his precious books to school and stored them in his third grade desk. That afternoon, after getting directions from me on how to get to the nearest equipment company, his teacher left school early to pick up a supply of backhoe books to continue Sonny's project.

As the years went on, Sonny graduated from backhoes to four-wheelers to pickups. Academics never came easy for him, but he made it through middle school. As soon as he was eligible, he enrolled in the high school vocational program and developed and practiced his skills in auto mechanics. Today he is studying and working a part-time job to help finance the pickup truck that he proudly owns.

My experience with Sonny taught me much more than I would ever have imagined, and I count myself fortunate that it came early in my career. It strongly supports my philosophy that all children can and do learn. I'm grateful to know the value of time and effort invested in finding a way to help a child. The learning button is always there. As teachers, we just have to identify it and gently push it.

RUTH FERRIS
Copper Canyon, Texas

A Good Kid

THURSDAY WAS A busy day. My general music classes started with a class of sixth graders, then fifth graders, followed by three classes of kindergarten children. After lunch, there were two first grade classes and two more kindergarten classes. Whew, lots of singing for one day!

During my final class that day, the children informed me that Kevin, the boy in chair fourteen, had been so bad that his teacher had taken him to the principal's office. "Oh my," I said, "I don't want to hear anything bad about any of you. You're all so special that if you must tell me something, I hope it will be something *good*." At our school, we put special emphasis on developing positive self concepts. Many of the songs we sing are songs that make children feel good about themselves, their neighbors, and the world they live in.

While they sang their next song, I went over to my class list to see if Kevin had a "G" next to his name. The "G" stood for

"Good Kid Award," an award I gave to two students during each class. I kept track so every child had a chance to receive one. I decided to watch Kevin. If he behaved, sang, and followed the rules, I would give him the award. He looked like he could use it.

When class was over that afternoon, I handed Kevin the "Good Kid Award." He was so pleased. He politely thanked me, and gave me a hug. The other children objected, however, saying that he had been bad in the other classroom. I replied that he had behaved in the music room, sang our songs, followed our rules, and therefore had earned the award.

Kevin's kindergarten teacher, Mrs. Munoz, was waiting at the door for her students. She explained to me that Kevin had indeed had a very bad morning. She mentioned that he was the oldest child in the room, and that he was bored with kindergarten work and needed to be moved to a first grade classroom. As I looked over the line of students, I noticed that Kevin was a whole head taller than most of the other children. Moments later, Mrs. Munoz and her class were on their way back to their classroom.

The alarm went off the next morning as usual. Because I was having car trouble, my husband dropped me off at school just after seven thirty, shortly before my eight o'clock breakfast duty. As I went up the ramp to my classroom, Mrs. Munoz started up after me. I wondered what she wanted.

"Are you coming to see me?"

"Yes," she replied. "I wanted to thank you for giving Kevin that award yesterday."

"Oh, that was no problem," I replied. "I thought he might need it."

Tears welled in her eyes.

"What's wrong?" I asked.

"Kevin drowned last night."

I was stunned.

I had heard a special bulletin on the morning news about a seven year old in our town who had drowned in an irrigation ditch after being tangled in debris. When the newscaster mentioned the child's name, however, I had been distracted.

Mrs. Munoz continued, "He had a really bad day yesterday, and I was so exasperated with him. After he got the award from you he was behaving much better, and I praised him before he left for home. I told him how proud I was of him. I'm so glad his school day ended on a positive note. I don't think I could have lived with myself otherwise." She left. I felt numb.

Later in the day, I spent a few silent moments thinking about Kevin and saying my good-byes to him. I was sorry I didn't have the chance to know him better, but I was pleased that I was able to contribute a small, positive moment to his young life.

Much of the time I wonder if what I'm doing really makes a difference. Most of the time, the answer isn't readily apparent. I rarely get feedback that lets me know I'm having an impact on the lives of the children I teach. But that day I think I was able to make a small difference.

EVY FULLER
Chandler, Arizona

Lessons Carved in Stone

*I*IDOLIZED MY high school biology teacher. Ed Mills made learning biology something special, and it was obvious that he found his work satisfying and fulfilling.

In the summers he and his family traveled to Yellowstone National Park, where he worked as a seasonal park ranger with the National Park Service. In his spare time, he officiated at basketball games in my hometown, Vandalia, Illinois. I admired him and wanted nothing more than a career similar to the one he so obviously enjoyed.

I trained to be a biology teacher in college, building on my long-time fascination with the outdoors. While student teaching as a senior in college, I discovered that I had chosen the right path—teaching punched my buttons. It was wonderful to share stories of the natural world with students, just as Mr. Mills had done with me. I planned to find a teaching job as soon as I graduated.

As fate would have it, however, I never made it to the classroom. Instead, I found a unique way to teach: first as an environmental educator at a camp, and later, as a park ranger. Eventually, I was hired as a park interpreter at Giant City State Park, just ten miles south of Carbondale, Illinois. As a park interpreter, my job was to teach natural and cultural history, work as manager of the visitors center, supervise programming for visiting school groups, and conduct programming for visitors. Nature was my classroom, and trail hikes, campfire activities, and special events were my programs.

I had much to learn about the history of the area, the Native Americans that lived there, and the ways that humans had changed the landscapes of the park. With more than one million visitors annually, my job at Giant City was unusually busy. I was teaching, provoking interest, revealing hidden meanings to my audiences; but not just about biology. Cultural history was just as important as the natural history of the park. The stories of people and resources were intertwined in every way.

One sunny Saturday, I led the weekly guided trail hike up into the narrow canyons of sandstone for which the park is named, the Giant City Nature Trail. Huge blocks of 200 million-year-old sandstone had slid apart on a foundation of shale to create cool, narrow canyons, often referred to as Streets of the Giants, festooned with ferns and mosses. My group for the day was typical, twenty-five or so parents with young children, empty nesters, and seniors, all clustered around stop number three, an Indian rock carving—one of my favorites. Physically, the face was just above waist height to an adult, carved on the square corner of a giant block of sandstone, evidence of an ancient river sandbar.

"What does this look like to you?" I asked.

"A face," someone answered.

"An Indian face!" another offered.

"Yes, it's a petroglyph, a carving on a rock. Do you see the feathers carved above the face?"

They did. I explained that an archaeologist told me that the carving of the face was probably one thousand years old or older, but the feathers were carved more recently. Someone who knew American Indians only from television had added them—an act of vandalism. The group was fascinated by the stone face, and I saw their imaginations spring to life as they gazed at the surroundings and wondered about the people who once lived in those beautiful woodlands among the cool bluffs. One young girl broke the trance, surprising me with her question.

"Where are the others?" she asked quietly.

"What others?" I responded, a little too quickly.

"There *must* be others. They wouldn't have made just one, would they?"

"In my five years of leading this trail," I pontificated, "I've never seen others."

She was sure I was wrong. I was certain I was right.

"Can I look for more of them?" she asked.

I was confident she would not succeed. "Sure, go ahead," I said thinking, "What can it hurt, there aren't any others."

The young lady walked the trail quietly, looking carefully at every wall of rock in the steep canyons of the trail. She found one face, more primitive than the first. Then she found another, and another. She seemed to find them easily as if they were messages, clearly left to speak to her. I was stunned. How had I missed these other faces during my hundreds of trips on the very same trail? Before we finished the one-mile hike, she'd found a total of four. She believed there were even more. She was right.

> *Education is not just what we learn in school. We have the opportunity to grow and become better communicators, partners, parents, teachers, students, and workers in everything we do.*

In the three years that followed, after exhaustive searches of the canyons and bluffs, I found three more. The young girl had opened my eyes, and now they seemed to be everywhere. Looking back, she taught me not to take familiar surroundings for granted. I realized how little I've learned from life's journey, and how little time there is to learn more.

Some time later, while training seasonal park interpreters for Illinois State Parks, I looked out at the audience of fifty eager workers, mostly college students. As I told the group about the man who had inspired my choice of career paths,

I saw a strong reaction—one of pride—in the face of one trainee. It was that of Ed Mills, my former teacher! He was working as a seasonal interpreter at a state park, while continuing to teach high school during the school year. Although I was surprised to see him, I was not surprised that he was still seeking opportunities to continue learning, while sharing his own knowledge. I was more than grateful to have the opportunity to thank him in front of a group of colleagues.

I now manage a nonprofit professional association for park interpreters throughout the world, and I occasionally teach at Colorado State University. I encourage students who love to learn to become teachers, and I remind them that there will always be lessons to learn from their students.

Education is not just what we learn in school. We have the opportunity to grow and become better communicators, partners, parents, teachers, students, and workers in everything we do. Self-education is a life-long task. There are always more faces to find along the trail. And there will always be new trails to walk.

TIM MERRIMAN
Fort Collins, Colorado

Tilman Speaks of Alligators

*T*ILMAN IS OUR class's newest arrival
fresh from the Liberian countryside.
School is new to him
and he is mystified by magnets
that hold various classroom artifacts
to the chalkboard
like pinned butterflies
caught mid-flight.

In the middle of the lesson
Tilman walks slowly to the board
as if transfixed.

He removes one of the magnets
turning it over and over

in his small, cracked palm
staring at it for code-breaking clues.

This process is re-enacted again
and again
and again
and Tilman looks surprised each time
the magnet repeats its "magic."

His mouth
the "O"-shape
of what I imagine the people look like
when making the "Wheel of Fortune" soundtrack.
You know, the sharp "Ews" and "Aws" that can
    be heard
when a contestant spins the wheel
and it lands on the $5,000 mark.

On his second day
Tilman ventures from the shadows during recess
to join his new classmates in a game of basketball.
When passed the ball
Tilman's eyes dart furtively from left to right.
Suddenly he dashes down the asphalt court
with the ball planted firmly in the crook of his
    right arm
like an NFL football player
going for the tie-breaking touchdown.

Even basketball
and the concept of dribbling
are new to Tilman.

I feel a shift
more in my stomach than my heart, really
and I don't know if I'm stifling laughter or tears,
possibly both.

Today
during third period
Tilman speaks of alligators.
"They are very bad," he says,
"They eat babies."
Tilman's accent is Liberian-thick
and I am unsure I have heard him correctly.
When asked what he means
Tilman calmly replies,
"In Liberia, people steal each other's babies
and throw them into the river.
The alligators usually get to them
before the people can. It is because of the war."

Tilman tires of talking alligators,
his attention suddenly shifting
to a classmate's sticker collection.
I hear the rise and fall of Tilman's voice
as he unsuccessfully barters his lunch

of stale bread and peanut butter
in exchange for two stickers.
He stares at Garfield and The Power Rangers
with ferocious yearning.

And once again
I feel like laughing
and crying
because today
it is Halloween
and I had been afraid to tell my students
a Halloween story
that might give them bad dreams.

I wonder
what could possibly frighten a child
who so matter-of-factly
recounts truthful stories
of baby-eating alligators
in a country full of war.

I MET TILMAN three years ago during my first year as an
ESOL (English for Speakers of Other Languages) teacher. Because of the war and caste system, Tilman did not attend school
in Liberia, his native country. In fact, Tilman had never set foot
in a classroom, held a pencil, or written his name on a piece of
paper until he started school in the United States at the age of
eleven. Needless to say, Tilman had a lot of catching up to do!

Like many of my other "ESOLers," his address changed frequently. As a result, it was difficult to keep track of him. After Tilman left our school, we stayed in touch primarily by phone. Tilman would call collect from a pay phone and we would talk about his new school, apartment, friends, and anything else of interest.

As Tilman's calls became shorter and less frequent, my concern for him grew. I worried about him surviving the rough neighborhoods he lived in. Being rather small for his age and having a pronounced accent didn't help Tilman blend in with the kids of his various neighborhoods. I worried about him falling in with the wrong crowd and succumbing to peer pressure. I worried about his low literacy skills. I worried about Tilman. I worried a lot.

I am happy to report that for the time being, my days of tracing Tilman's travels on the map are over. Tilman and his family recently returned to Maryland. More importantly, Tilman is safe, sound, and successful! He is currently attending one of the neighborhood high schools. He visits me after school in the library quite frequently, sometimes as often as three times a week! Sometimes I help Tilman with his homework. Sometimes we simply talk. We talk about school, family, how to make a good impression in a job interview, future personal and professional goals, and more.

Tilman visits until it is time to collect his four younger siblings from the local elementary school. After walking them home and preparing their afternoon snack, Tilman does the family grocery shopping. He then walks to one of his part-time jobs. After work, Tilman returns home, eats dinner, and completes his homework. Both of Tilman's parents work multiple jobs. Whichever parent is home supervises Tilman as he studies. Then it is time to go to sleep and rest well for the following day; another day filled with responsibilities most children in this country could not comprehend, much less shoulder.

Amazingly, Tilman never complains. He says he is happy to help his family. He is happy to contribute financially; happy to help care for his younger siblings, happy to forgo the things that most American teenagers live for—dances, sports, and hanging out at the mall.

There are very few things I claim to be certain of. However, in a few short years, I'm certain that I'll to be standing and applauding in a crowded high school auditorium while Tilman, diploma in hand, proudly crosses the stage, facing the audience and world with pride, promise, determination, and integrity. I am overjoyed that this young man has the opportunity to live in a society where he no longer has to worry about alligators. I am certain Tilman's life and the life of his children will be a good one.

FELICIA L. MORGENSTERN
Colombia, Maryland

Gifts from the Heart

*A*s I was sorting through some boxes this summer, I came across a brown one labeled, "M. H. Third Grade." My daughter came into the room. She knelt down beside me.

"What's in the box, Mom?" she asked as she lifted the tattered lid. Inside was a small, broken child's tea cup and saucer; an ink pen; a dirty, dingy, white hair bow; a pair of soiled arm sweat bands; and an apple-shaped pencil holder that read, "#1 Teacher" on the front.

"Why are you keeping all this nasty, broken stuff? It looks like a pile of trash," my daughter said.

"Oh, this isn't trash, honey. These are treasures from the hearts of some of my most precious students," I replied as I let myself slip back into time.

We had just moved to a new town because of my husband's job. I was the new teacher on the block, and a common policy in education is giving the new teacher a class that she'll never forget—if she lives through it.

I was given a remedial third grade class. That was fine with me. I'd taught second grade for four years, so I didn't expect it to be too much of an adjustment. I began to have serious doubts, however, during my preplanning when the teachers from down the hall would stop by my room, shut the door, and tell me how sorry they were that I was getting so-and-so from her class. Some even left in tears letting me know that, for the record, they had nothing to do with setting up my class. Young, naive, and somewhat spoiled from teaching at a wonderful country school, I thought I could handle anything. How bad could it be? Hadn't I already dealt with behavior problems in the past? I'd show them! Those kids would be eating out of my hand in no time at all.

I greeted each of my new students on the first day of school. In walked the biggest third graders I'd ever seen. Donte, weighing in at 225 pounds, could easily have made the first string on a high school football team. He looked me straight in the eye with a glare that said, "I hate school and you can't make me learn." Sedrick, tall and lanky with an attitude in tow, looked down at me. His favorite words for the year turned out to be "I can't do that," delivered in a long drawn-out whine. I began to get nervous as more children began to saunter into the classroom. With the exception of two bright-eyed and innocent-looking girls, all the kids seemed troubled, old for their grade, and full of anger.

Latikka, the thief, stole from everyone, including me. Fawn, the informer, brought a box of condoms to school and passed them out with verbal instructions. David, the fighter, brought in a knife to kill Sedrick because Sedrick had said something about his mama. Lindsay, the quiet one, cowered in the corner, hardly ever saying a word, which was probably not a bad idea considering the possible risks. Sean, the doctor's child, was loud, obnoxious, and always saying mean insulting remarks about everyone in the class. To describe him as hyperactive would be an understatement.

My delusions of grandeur dissolved instantly. From that day forward, I left school crying and exhausted from the stress of just trying to keep the kids from killing me or each other.

As time went on, I discovered that every child, except for two of them, had been retained at least one grade-level. In fact, most had been retained every year since kindergarten. The majority were twelve or thirteen years old and still in the third grade, although most were academically functioning below first-grade level when they started their year with me. The only exceptions were the two girls who, although in the gifted program, were inexplicably assigned to my classroom. They were clearly out of place and terrified by the other students.

Determined, I went all the way back to pull from my kindergarten and first grade teaching experiences. I used manipulatives for teaching math and learning centers for social skills. I read from every good literature book that I could find on their level. We also began journal writing. I realized that these kids needed much more than academic skills—they needed love, compassion, and patience. We worked on attitude and self-esteem. Every morning I told them that they were intelligent and wonderful kids. I told them how proud I was to have them in my class. I focused only on their strengths, ignoring everything but weapons and physical assaults. We role played ways to work through conflicts and wrote about our feelings. Over time, we read lots and lots of books. We wrote pages and pages in our journals.

By December, I was beginning to see an improvement in their attitudes and behavior. For every day that we made it without major disruptions, I rewarded them with little prizes. If we made it for a week, I had a class cooking activity. Those kids loved to eat!

As the week before Christmas break arrived, there was a noticeable change in some of the students. They seemed more negative and quick-tempered. We talked about the coming holidays. They appeared extremely interested in what I would be doing. I talked about my children and our family get-together. I told them about going home to my parents' house and opening gifts with the family. The more I talked, the quieter the class became. Suddenly, I realized what a fool I'd been. Many of these kids didn't share similar holiday experiences. Their homes were often not warm and caring, gifts were not abundant, food not plentiful. Finally, Lindsay, the quiet one, asked if I was going to give them a gift.

"Yes, of course," I replied. Sam asked what I wanted for Christmas. Latikka asked if I was going to be mad at her because she couldn't buy me anything. Others joined in with their concerns. It occurred to me that these kids were worrying about me! They were upset because they couldn't afford to buy me a gift.

I told them that I loved cards and letters more than anything. I set aside time for them to create special cards for me to be opened at our party the Friday before the Christmas break. The mood of the class picked up considerably. Small groups gathered in whispers and soon everyone had projects going.

On the day of our party, everyone came together for the gift opening activities. I gave each of them a children's book, a new journal, and a pencil decorated with holiday images. The children gathered around as I began to read the cards they had made. It was hard to choke back the tears as I read each special message—every one deeply meaningful and from the heart. As Lindsay handed me her card, she also handed me a small object wrapped in toilet paper and paper towels. Inside was a broken child's tea cup and saucer. She said it was her favorite and that she had found it when she was little. She wanted me to have it for my morning coffee. Sandy handed me a gift wrapped in paper recycled from the books I had given them earlier. Inside was a white bow for my hair. It was soiled from lots of wear and the ends were frayed. I told her I would save it to wear for special occasions. Sam handed me an unwrapped red, apple-shaped pencil holder that read, "#1 Teacher" on the front. His mom had taken him to the flea market and he spent his saved-up allowance on it. He beamed as he handed it to me. Finally, Latikka handed me a gift wrapped in construction paper from the art table. As I unrolled the paper, a blue, expensive Cross pen rolled out. It was the same pen she had stolen from me earlier in the year. She told me how she had bought it from a local store, and of course, I said, "Thank you." I was, after all, grateful to have it back.

As usual, I went home and cried. But this time was different. I cried because of the love that these children had demonstrated in the best way that they could: by giving me gifts from their hearts—gifts I will treasure forever.

ALISA DANIEL
Sylvania, Georgia

Celebrate the Differences

*I*T WAS A hot, humid September morning when I reported to my first day of third grade—in a new school. Only weeks before this frightful day I had been playing with my two best friends in my backyard in Michigan. How I needed to be back there with Jeannie and Pam once again.

Father explained to my sister and I that he had taken an exciting new job in Philadelphia, and we had to move before school started. At first the idea sounded exciting to me, but not after I realized I wouldn't be playing with my best friends any more. I wasn't even sure where Philadelphia was, but I knew it would definitely be far away and lonely.

My mother walked the block and a half with me to Central School, on that first morning, to make sure I knew the route. She kissed me goodbye and wished me luck.

I walked down the long, noisy hallway until I saw room 355. I stood in the doorway and looked around. Nothing in my young life had prepared me for what I was about to see. Miss Tillman, my tall and rather matronly teacher, was missing her left arm. The left sleeve of her very sheer, long-sleeved blouse was fastened securely to her waist by a thin belt. She was greeting the students as they entered her classroom. I froze in the doorway, my feet glued to the floor. I knew I had to move but I didn't know where to go first. Part of me wanted to go running back home.

"My name is Miss Tillman. And what is your name young lady?" The teacher asked as she walked toward me. I swallowed a few times before choking out, "Laura. . . . My name is Laura . . . Hayes." Then came the part I dreaded. "You are our new student aren't you?" she inquired. "Please come over here and sit next to Tim." She pulled my chair out with her right arm and then motioned for me to be seated. In order for her to accomplish this task Miss Tillman had to lean over me, allowing her left sleeve to brush against my face. I was horrified to receive a ghastly view of her stump through the thin fabric.

It was, however, a relief to be assigned to the back row. The sight of a one-armed teacher was scary enough at a distance, and I prayed she would never come close to me again.

I looked around the huge classroom filled with total strangers as I felt the muggy air strangling me. Miss Tillman passed out the usual—books, paper, crayons, pencils, and glue. She told us about her classroom rules and gave us important instructions about going to the cafeteria and fire drill procedures. After what seemed like forever, we were finally dismissed for recess.

Recess was awful! Not one person wanted to play with me on the playground. I was extremely shy, and besides that, everyone already had their own friends from last year. I took the easy way out by sitting alone on a swing. Without anyone to talk to, anyone to play with, I felt terribly alone. I wished Pam and Jeannie could be there. When I was with them I didn't feel alone at all.

When we returned to the classroom, Miss Tillman gave us the ever-popular back-to-school assignment: Write an essay on "What I Did During My Summer Vacation." I took a pencil in hand and started writing, an activity I was confident about and loved to do. I was anxious to put down on paper all of my feelings of the last several traumatic weeks.

Our desks were arranged together in groups of six—three facing three—pushed together to make a large square. As the papers were being collected, I noticed that the other children had written their essays using fancy penmanship! "Oh no!" I thought. I'd simply printed mine! Because of our desk arrangements, the other students could see that I wasn't only new, I was *different*—my paper was the only one that was printed. Now everyone would know that the new kid didn't know how to write! I wondered if I'd ever make friends now. I also wondered what Miss Tillman would say when she saw it.

Miss Tillman proceeded to guide us through the remainder of the day. My eyes became accustomed to her different appearance, and soon I stopped looking at the arm she didn't have. I concentrated on her soft voice, unique facial expressions, and the two dimples that appeared every time she smiled. No matter what she talked about, she made it sound fascinating.

Over the next several days, I managed to make a new friend and began to feel better about my new school, but on Friday afternoon, our essays were returned. Giggles of delight echoed throughout the classroom as the grades were revealed. I held my breath as I looked at my paper. It contained a special message across the top, written in red ink: "Please see me after class." My heart stopped, and I prayed that the floor would open up and swallow me whole. The embarrassment of having to stay after school was overwhelming, not to mention my fear: Was I in trouble because I didn't know how to write in cursive?

After the classroom was empty, I looked toward Miss Tillman. "Laura, please come over here."

I didn't want to go, but I knew I had to, so I got up and approached her desk.

"I have noticed that you aren't like the other students—you are different," she said.

"I don't want to be *different*," I thought to myself. "I want to be like everyone else!" But, before I could dwell on her comment too long, she continued.

"You are different in that you have a talent for writing, and I can see by your essay that you have some writing experience.

So, now it's time to learn penmanship like a real author. I have something special for you," she said and handed me a book on penmanship. "Which hand do you write with dear?"

Surprised, I stammered, "My, uh, my left hand ma'am."

Miss Tillman's two dimples appeared as she laughed and looked down at her left-sided stump. "Well," she smiled, "I wouldn't be a very good teacher for this lesson, would I? Is there someone at home who could help you over the weekend?"

I relaxed a little. "I could ask Mom," I said hopefully. "She has lovely handwriting."

"Your mother is it then. Use this book to help you and come back on Monday to show me how well you can write. Oh, and by the way—for your candor, you got an A+!"

"Yes Ma'am," I said quickly, ending with, "Thank you." I didn't know what *candor* was, but I was happy about my A+! I took the book and started to pack my school bag. I was almost ready to leave the classroom when Miss Tillman came to my desk. She sat in the chair across from mine and spoke in a soft, clear voice.

"You have noticed that I am different. Most people look at the arm that I no longer have before they look at me to see who I really am. The accident that took my arm changed my life in an instant and made me different . . . unique . . . forever. It was then that I decided to be the best teacher that I could possibly be. To make a difference in this world."

She stood up, walked me to the door, and continued. "All of us are different in some way, and for some of us the difference is more obvious. Laura, you too are different, but differences aren't always bad. You have special gifts. Be proud of who you are and dare to use your talents—all of them."

THE REMAINDER OF that school year sailed past all too quickly. I began to build self-confidence and feel good about myself, I learned how to write, and eventually, I outgrew my shyness. Thanks to Miss Tillman, a part of me was forever changed because she taught me the most important lessons I would ever learn: Respect the differences in others, feel proud about the things that make you unique, and use your gifts to help others. If you live by these rules, you can't go wrong.

LAURA LAGANA
Wilmington, Delaware

View from Down Under

$\mathcal{A}$s an educational advisor in North Queensland, Australia, I was often called on to assist classroom teachers with specific problems. I particularly remember one request from a second-year teacher who was having trouble teaching mathematics to her aboriginal students.

After a long drive along dusty roads, I arrived at the school and spent some time discussing with the teacher the aspects of math the children were having trouble with. She talked for a long time explaining in vague terms, "They just don't get it."

"Give me a specific example of what they don't get," I prompted.

"Okay," she said. "Our math syllabus suggests that the students should be able to classify objects. So the other day, I took out the colored blocks and demonstrated how they can be sorted into shapes, sizes, or colors—you know the routine," she sighed.

"So what happened?" I asked.

"Well, then I asked them to begin the activity, but they just didn't get it. They sorted the blocks every which way and the whole lesson was just a mess. I became so frustrated that I ended up yelling at the kids."

"Okay," I said. "Let's go down to the classroom and try this again in a different way."

As we reached the classroom the children were just returning from recess. They were a lively bunch with beautiful smiles and warm natures. They immediately wanted to know who I was and why I was there.

After giving them the information they needed, I suggested we go outside and collect some things and bring them back to the classroom.

We all trudged outside into the bright sunshine. I carried a bucket and instructed the children to collect things that were growing. We very quickly had a variety of different leaves, grasses, and blossoms.

We returned to the classroom and sat in a circle while I emptied the contents of the bucket onto the carpet.

"Let's see how we can sort these," I said as I began to put all the leaves in one pile, all the grasses in another, and the blossoms in a third. "Have a look at these three piles," I said. "Why do you think I have arranged them like this?"

Twenty pairs of eyes stared back at me and there was silence for what seemed an eternity. Then Joseph slowly raised his hand. "There isn't no reason to put 'em like that Miss 'cause they all grow'n things and that don't make sense puttin' them like that!"

I began to feel the frustration that the classroom teacher had described, and as I looked toward her I could see she was wearing a smug look that said, "I told you so."

My mind raced as to what to do next when I remembered a highly respected educator saying to me, "If the teacher can't teach the learner, get the learner to teach the teacher."

I pushed the objects together into the middle of the circle and said, "Okay. See if you can trick me; put these things into families and then I'll try to guess how you've done it.

I will never forget what happened next. Not a word was spoken between the twenty children but there must have been a wealth of nonverbal communication going on. After about three minutes of silent shuffling and moving of the objects, twenty faces sat back and looked at me expectantly.

I gazed at the three piles the children had placed on the carpet and could see no reason for them to be grouped in that way. In my head, I quickly ran through all the physical attributes I could think of—color, size, shape —but nothing seemed to fit.

Puzzled and deflated, I looked at the group and spoke tentatively, "I don't know why you've grouped them like this. I'm afraid you'll have to tell me. What about you Janice? Can you explain it to me?"

"It's easy Miss," responded Janice. "See these ones here? They got a real strong smell." She pointed to the pile nearest to her. "And see this pile here Miss? They got a little bit of a smell, and this other lot here, they got no smell at all."

I felt a light bulb go off in my head and I was anxious to see if the process could work again.

"Very good," I said. "Do you think you could do that again in another way?" Twenty curly black heads nodded and after another three minutes of silent moving and shuffling, the class sat back smiling at me, knowing that they were going to trick me again.

After a few feeble (and wrong) guesses, I gave up and asked for an explanation of the two piles.

Joseph explained, "See this lot here Miss, they grow first when the wet season comes and this pile here, they grow later, when the real heavy rains come."

I repeated the process with the class about five or six times, and each time the students were able to show that they had highly developed classifying skills—skills that demonstrated a connectedness to *their* way of life, not mine. I realized the richness and importance of giving children the opportunity to think in different ways.

These children taught me that there are always new perspectives—new ways of looking at things—and you should keep your mind open to *all* possibilities. They also taught me that, as a teacher, you must always be prepared to become a learner. These two priceless lessons have continued to shape and guide my career as an educator.

DOT WALKER
Queensland, Australia

A Night to Remember

I'VE PLAYED MANY roles as an educator these past thirty-five years, but I played one of my most memorable roles just last year when I seized the opportunity to be a prom queen. Yes, it would appear that I'm a bit old for that role, but one never knows what surprises will pop up when you're an educator. It all began last April with an unexpected phone call.

"Hi, is this Ms. Wright?" an unfamiliar voice asked.

"Yes it is, who's calling?" I responded.

"Ms. Wright, this is T.C. Randolph. I work for the school district as a social worker on behalf of homeless kids and kids who live in group homes. We're looking for an 'angel' and your name was given to me by someone in my office."

"Is that so?" I exclaimed, wondering what new adventures this angel solicitation would bring to my life.

"Well," he continued, "many of the kids with whom I work attend alternative or continuation school programs, and unfortunately our school district has never appropriated funds for these schools to have a prom. It would be so wonderful if you or someone you know could help us put together a prom this year."

Without hesitating, I enthusiastically replied, "You've got it, T.C.!" Frankly, I'm not sure how those words slipped out of my mouth so quickly. I guess for a brief moment I thought about how important proms are in the lives of high school juniors and seniors. It seemed unfair that these inner-city students, many of whom led troubled lives, would be cheated out of this experience. As it turned out, my impromptu reply was the beginning of an astounding and memorable adventure!

T.C. and I continued the conversation, and by the time it ended, I'd agreed to work with student and staff representatives from the various schools and financially sponsor the prom. The shock came later when I realized I had made a major commitment without a clue as to how much time and money this project would require. Nonetheless, the following week, I met with ten students and four staff members from the various continuation schools. I facilitated the first meeting by asking questions of the students: "What kind of prom do you want? What kind of music would you like? What about food?" As they were answering the questions it became clear that I wouldn't want this prom to take place in a rented hall or church basement with home-cooked chicken.

This had to be a *great* prom. It was after all the very first continuation school prom in the history of the school district. As the meeting progressed, I asked the students to come up with a "theme." A lovely Hispanic girl named Alicia smiled and said, "Let's call it, 'A Night to Remember.'"

"Perfect," I replied. "Then let's make sure this indeed turns out to be a night to remember. How would you like to have your prom on a yacht, a chartered yacht with dinner and a great DJ playing your favorite music?" I saw their faces light up.

"Really? You mean we can have the prom on a boat and sail around the Bay?"

"Why not," I replied, "If that's what you want, that's what you'll have."

We were all so excited about the yacht idea that once again, I didn't stop to think about the financial consequences of my promise. In that moment, nothing mattered except the bright, smiling faces of the young people who were now officially designated "the prom committee."

Upon gathering information about the yacht, dinner, and DJ expenses, I realized the necessity of requesting financial support from my friends and family in order to cover the now exorbitant cost of the prom. I sent out letters describing the project and asked them to open their hearts and wallets. Amazingly, they came through! Friends who lived thousands of miles away donated money. Ex-boyfriends sent checks. My relatives in Southern California participated. I was inspired by the willingness of so many people to help make this prom a reality!

Although the budgeting aspect of the project was turning out well, there was another major challenge to deal with—one that I hadn't considered, but one that could have had serious repercussions. At one of the prom committee meetings, I was informed that two of the continuation schools had rival gang members who wouldn't even ride on the same public bus or walk on the same street as the other. Students and staff on the committee felt we should invite one, but not both of the schools. The school district administrator however, was adamant that if this was a continuation school prom, we'd have to invite *all* the continuation schools.

I recall the look of panic and despair on the faces of the prom committee members when I told them we had to include students from both schools. They responded by describing all the possible violent scenarios that would occur: We might have a riot on the yacht in the middle of the Bay; someone might get stabbed or shot; someone might get thrown overboard and drown. While they spoke, I felt my stomach tightening as I imagined the horrors the students were describing. But I had already paid a hefty non-refundable deposit for the yacht, and the flyers had already been printed and distributed. We were going to have a prom regardless of who showed up, including the rival gang members. We were going to have to figure out how to keep it free of violence. We definitely had our work cut out for us.

I have to admit I didn't sleep well for weeks before the prom night. An evening spent amongst rival gang members was terribly risky, and I wasn't sure that I was prepared for it. I found myself agonizing over the possibility that I could be responsible for some parent's son or daughter being injured or killed. I was worried about liability—my own, as well as the school district's. This could indeed become a night to remember, but for reasons completely different than we originally thought.

The prom committee and I did everything possible to prevent the predicted nightmare. We had students and their parents or guardians sign agreements that prom participants would not have weapons, alcohol, or drugs in their possession. We hired off-duty policemen who would search the students as they boarded the yacht, and we made sure the DJ and prom security staff were big fellows who could handle any fights that might occur. We also arranged for twenty teachers (and their guests) to attend the prom, as well as the administrators of the various schools. And then I prayed. I prayed that all the work the prom committee did, would not be in vain. I prayed that the people who generously donated money for this project would not be disappointed, and I prayed that the students would be on their best behavior and make this a wonderful and extraordinary evening. Yes, I prayed for a miracle.

For one incredible evening, they forgot about gangs and rivalry. They forgot they lived in housing projects and group homes.

Finally the long-awaited night arrived. And they came— almost two hundred of them, decked out in their finest prom wear. Some wore borrowed clothes, others wore suits and dresses they had spent weeks saving and searching for. They all looked so beautiful! And wow, were they excited! A good number of these inner-city teenagers had never been on a boat of any kind, and here they were boarding a yacht! They enjoyed the wonderful gourmet dinner, took photos of each other, and danced up a storm throughout the evening. But they didn't fight, and they didn't riot. For one incredible evening, they forgot about gangs and rivalry. They forgot they lived in housing projects and group homes. They forgot they were considered the school district "troublemakers" and "losers." What they remembered, it seems, is that they were beautiful, proud young men and women who deserved as much as anyone to have an elegant prom.

As for me, I was the happiest and proudest unofficial prom queen that ever lived! Because of the success of our prom, I am confident that there will be many more continuation school proms in this school district. Although they may not take place on a chartered yacht, they will be wonderful, nonetheless. And, I have no doubt that each and every one will become a night to remember.

ESTHER WRIGHT
San Francisco, California

Planting Seeds of Love

*I*T HAS BEEN my good fortune over the past three and a half years to have the privilege of working with a group of Latino parents whose children attend schools in our district. Nearly all of them are Mexican, and the great majority are employed in some type of agricultural work. Although these parents were once in the migrant stream, they have since settled in Oregon's Willamette Valley.

Even though their children are learning English in school, most of these parents are still extremely limited in their own English proficiency. Because of this, few members of our community share my good fortune in getting to know who these individuals are, and the great wealth of knowledge that they bring with them.

The wealth of knowledge that they possess is not necessarily knowledge in the academic sense of the word. Because of the economic realities of life in Mexico, many were not able to pursue an education beyond elementary school. Some even have limited literacy skills in their mother tongue and struggle to read the children's books in Spanish that make up the backbone of our family literacy project, *Libros y Familias* (Books and Families). Yet I have learned more from these parents than I have from many professors whose offices were decked with a plethora of degrees and diplomas from prestigious institutions of higher learning. The diplomas of these parents are from the "School of Life," and are not displayed on office walls, but engraved in their hands and faces. Were I to compare our educations, I seriously question whether I could pass the tests that they have passed or overcome the obstacles that they have overcome.

The reason that I remain in the teaching profession has nothing to do with state standards or test scores. In fact it has little to do with the academic side of teaching. It has much more to do with the realm of feelings and emotions. I feel that the most important service that I have rendered is not teaching people to read, write, and do mathematical operations. As important as these skills are, there are many people who can teach them better than I can. I stay in teaching because of the human aspect, the caring and sharing side that is seldom assessed or evaluated by our educational system, and for which no state or national standards have been developed.

For the past twelve years, I have worked with language minority students and their families, both at the elementary and secondary levels. During that time I have found that what these individuals need most is to be understood and respected for who they are and what they have lived. This was a prerequisite to academic learning. I have shared in the pain that engulfed a Cambodian teenager who lost his mother and his sister when he fled his homeland, and I've comforted a young Mexican high school student whose father died of cancer shortly after arriving in the United States. I have read student journals that cried for help, not to pass a test, but to survive the moment in a new culture. What more meaningful reason is there to write than to pour out your soul and try to make meaning of where life has taken you?

My most recent experience with Latino parents has allowed me to grapple more intimately with the inequities in our educational and social systems. The words that they have written or spoken have made it even clearer to me why I am in education. I refrain from saying why I teach, because I am the learner more often than I am the teacher.

Each month, we ask parents to respond, in writing, to a theme presented by a particular children's book. We've been publishing their words for the past three and a half years. Some of these words are written by the parents themselves and others are scribed for them. Regardless of how the words get on the page, they are always unpretentious, sincere, and to the point. The words on the page mirror the feelings within, reflecting the transformative and humanitarian aspects of education. They prove that learning does not occur only within school walls and that intelligence and wisdom transcend economic and class boundaries. Their words are amongst the reasons why I am still in education.

It is the hope of each of these parents that their children will have the opportunity to live a fruitful and satisfying life, with fewer hardships and a better education than they themselves had. They will not accept that their children's hands and minds are schooled for picking lettuce. As one mother wrote,

> *La voz que los maestros pueden tener e influir grandamente en los jovenes para la transformación del mundo. Maestros, a sembrar semillas de amor y esperanza verdaderos, tener responsibilidad auténtica.*

> *The voice that teachers have can have an enormous influence on our youth, who are capable of transforming this world. Teachers—to plant true seeds of love and hope, you have a genuine responsibility.*

It is that desire to plant true seeds of love and hope that bring me to teach. Teaching is one way to make a difference, to touch one or many in a manner that will make the world a better place. In doing so, I reap as much, if not more, than I have sown. I can't think of a better way to spend a life.

DICK KEIS
Corvallis, Oregon

Loose Change

*T*o say that Matt was a demanding first grader is an understatement! He was so desperate for attention that he would throw chairs, yell, "I hate you!" and bolt out of the classroom at various times throughout the day. During one memorable tantrum he blurted, "Did you know that my Mom's going to be fired because of the *loose change?*"

Puzzled by this mysterious comment, I contacted Matt's mother later in the day to gain some clarification. She confided that her job as a high school cafeteria worker was on the line because she had difficulty counting money and giving correct change. Although my days were filled with teaching and my nights were often spent grading papers or developing lesson plans, something in my heart told me I needed to find the time to help Matt's mom.

My tutoring sessions with Matt's mom began soon after that. We met several afternoons a week in my classroom and worked on the values of coins while Matt played with puzzles and games. A thin layer of ice began to trickle off Matt soon after the tutoring sessions began. At first, he didn't sit with us as we worked, but as the sessions continued, he began to inch his way closer to our table, all the while feigning disinterest. Before long, Matt's mother progressed to role-playing activities using the high school lunch menu. Eventually, Matt joined us, taking on the role of a student purchasing lunch. I was thrilled watching Matt and his mom work together and proud of the progress that both were making. Uncharacteristically, Matt began to smile and I discovered for the first time that he had wonderful dimples!

Matt's mother did not lose her job. We continued the money counting sessions for several weeks, and I was amazed to note the continued improvements in Matt's behavior during school. The tantrums became less frequent, and he spoke, rather than yelled, during class time. In short, Matt seemed like an entirely different child.

I knew that my time spent with Matt's mother was well worth it; there was a sense of accomplishment and satisfaction on her part as well as mine. But the coup de grace came the day I found a crumpled wad of paper on my desk. I opened the paper and smoothed out the wrinkles, instantly recognizing the printing. It read, "Did you know that I love you now? Matt."

PATTI SAPP
Bowie, Maryland

A Star Named Russell

ROM THE CLASSROOM window I could see dark storm clouds rolling in over the Wisconsin farm fields. My sixth period students were fidgeting nervously at their desks expecting a vocabulary test. I strolled over to the door, smiled, and dramatically switched off the lights. The dim room instantly fell silent.

"The test is canceled!" I announced. "In honor of Halloween, let's tell ghost stories instead!"

The kids, of course, hooted and hollered their surprise and before long we were all caught up in homespun versions of "The Monkey's Paw," "The Hitchhiker in the White Dress," and several enthusiastic versions of "The Killer with a Hook Instead of an Arm."

Then Mary, a wide-eyed cheerleader, raised her hand. "Do you think it's possible to communicate with someone who's dead?" Of course, every ear in the place perked up as I paused a moment before answering.

"Well, Mary, that's a good question. People have wondered about that for centuries. I don't know the answer, but I do believe we should try to keep an open mind about these things."

"I believe it's possible!" declared Russell Bray, the blonde boy in the varsity letter jacket. Every head turned toward him. He continued.

"It's like that book we read in here." Russell was referring to *The Little Prince,* a novel by Antoine de Saint Exuperey. "If you really love somebody, like that pilot loved the prince, you'll always stay connected, no matter what."

I had to smile. The entire class was a teacher's dream, but it was Russell who was the star. A blue-eyed junior, Russell was one of the most popular kids at Elkhorn High School and it wasn't hard to figure out why. He was just as apt to flash a friendly grin at a shy freshman girl as he was to his buddies on the varsity football team. He was never too cool to open a door for a teacher or too busy to muck out his family's dairy barn. In fact, he raised prize-winning calves in 4-H, never missed football practice, and still managed to stay on the honor roll. Now he was leaning forward in his desk flashing that trademark grin.

"Well, if I die before you do, Mrs. Madden, I promise to communicate, to give you some sign that I'm still around." At that very moment the autumn wind howled through the open window, fluttering the curtains and blowing a stack of papers off my desk. Someone screamed and then, a second later, we all burst out laughing.

"Oh, Russell, don't say that!" I protested. "You're sixteen and I'm twenty-six. I'll probably die before you anyway."

"Maybe," he said. "But just in case I die first, promise to watch for me, Okay?"

Of course, I promised.

Just before school let out that spring, I bought a box of old-fashioned gold stars to glue next to my faculty picture in the kids' yearbooks. My students had often teased me about my passion for the little foil stars and this was my way of saying good-bye to them before resigning and moving on to an English position at another school district. I also tried to write something personal in each student's yearbook by borrowing quotations from various books we had read together in class. In Russell's yearbook I paraphrased *The Little Prince:*

Whenever I see the wheat fields I will think of you, Russell, because your hair is the color of wheat. I think we all tamed each other this year; we established ties. You remind me of The Little Prince because you understand that what is essential is invisible to the eye.

Love & Gold Stars,
Mrs. Madden

The last day of school my sixth period class surprised me with a good-bye gift and a handmade card decorated with gold stars. Everyone wrote a message, including Russell, who chose, not surprisingly, a quotation from *The Little Prince:*

> *In one of the stars I shall be living. In one I shall be laughing. And so it will be as if all the stars were laughing, when you look at the sky at night. You—only you— will have stars that can laugh!*
>
> *Thanks for everything,*
> *Russell*

Although I was teaching in a different county the next fall, I heard from a friend that Russell, by then a senior, was suffering from mysterious headaches that had, at least on one occasion, sent him to the hospital. I sent him a get well card with a photograph of a wheat field on the front and congratulated him for being elected to homecoming court. It was only a week or two later that I got the phone call from a friend who taught at the high school.

"Patricia, I thought you should know that Russell died yesterday." The rest of the conversation became a blur, but I managed to absorb the most important parts. Russell had been practicing for the last football game of the season when a teammate tackled him. He stumbled, fell, got up, shook his head, and collapsed. By the time the ambulance arrived, he had slipped into a coma from which he never awoke. Russell died at the age of seventeen. His parents, though devastated, were deeply religious people and tried to accept Russell's death as God's will.

Doctors did not perform an autopsy, but speculated that Russ died of a brain aneurysm.

I took the day off to go to the funeral. It was held in a small brick church just off the town square. Hundreds of friends, farmers, and fellow classmates came to honor the golden boy of Elkhorn, Wisconsin. People overflowed from the church, down the steps, and onto the sidewalk. It was a crowd only fitting, of course, for a prince. Russell's parents met me at the front door, their faces gaunt with grief.

"Russ really liked your class," his father told me. "Sometimes he would talk to me about those books of yours while he milked the cows."

"I hope you don't mind," said Mrs. Bray, "but the minister is going to read what you wrote to Russ in his yearbook as the text for his sermon. I think Russ would like that."

So the same words that I had written so cheerfully the spring before were repeated now for Russell's eulogy. Later that afternoon, Russell Bray was buried in a country cemetery surrounded by wheat fields.

For weeks after the funeral I could not stop thinking of Russell and the promise he had made to me in the presence of his classmates: "If I die before you do, Mrs. Madden, I promise to communicate, to give you some sign that I'm still around." It was a terribly difficult time for me. Not only was I grieving over the tragic death of a gifted and gentle-hearted student, but I was also struggling with my own spiritual beliefs. How could the God of my childhood allow Russell to die so young? Was there a divine plan for each of us or was Russell's death a cruel accident? I, of course, remained both frightened and fascinated at the thought of Russell's promise and found myself sometimes actually talking to him out loud. "I'm not quite ready, Russell," I would say whenever the house seemed too dark or too quiet. "I'm not up to it now."

One cold and clear December night my husband and I drove up our dark country lane toward town. We had only gone about one-half mile when the car started thumping and bumping. There we were with a flat tire, no spare in the trunk, and friends expecting us for dinner. My husband volunteered to walk back to the house and get our truck so we wouldn't be late for dinner. I sat alone in the car and watched him disappear into the shadows. We had stopped on a hill near the pasture and I could see our horse grazing peacefully in the moonlight. Suddenly, an overwhelming sense of serenity overcame me and I heard myself say aloud, "Okay, Russell, I'm ready now. I need to know. Where are you? Are you okay?"

I don't really know what I expected, but I did know it was time to put this all to rest. And then, out of the corner of my eye, I saw a flash of amber. It was a brilliant shooting star, the most amazing one I had ever seen blazing across the whole horizon. I watched it soar up into the eastern sky, flare across the north, and flicker, finally, in the west. *In one of the stars I shall be living*, Russell had written on my good-bye card. *In one I shall be laughing.*

And that was the night (at least for me) when the stars began to laugh.

IT HAS BEEN twenty five years since Russell's death. I have since remarried and taught in three different states. My students sometimes tease me about my eclectic collection of gold stars. I even have a "star basket" for special awards. And once a year, usually around Christmas, I tell my students about a star named Russell.

PATRICIA J. ST. JOHN
Novato, California

Teacher's Report Card

I READ THE student evaluations with shock and dismay. I thought I had done a fine job teaching my first Management Communications class to adult students at the University of Calgary, but was saddened to see some of my students felt otherwise.

There was no mistaking the computer printout. The responses to "Rate the teaching in this course" showed that I had scored 3.7 out of 5.0. With an approval rating of 74% I was a "B" teacher; not the "A" teacher I aspired to be. On several points, a number of students had "strongly disagreed" with my methods.

The written comments gave me some insight into what the students felt I had done wrong. "We're not children!" one of the rating sheets admonished. "Don't treat us like we are." It was true. I had imposed a lot of rules and regulations on my adult students. I took attendance at every class, deducted points for late assignments, gave detailed criticism about what they had done wrong on their essay assignments, and required them to participate in every class activity for full marks. But wasn't discipline necessary to keep a class under control? You can't please everyone, I thought. Besides, what did my students know about teaching?

As I began to seriously reevaluate my teaching methods, I thought back to my own experiences as a student, and I remembered Mr. Chalmers.

Long before I became an instructor myself, I observed that Mr. Chalmers, my favorite and most influential teacher, had been very flexible. He had been willing to bend the rules if it meant a student would learn more, and he even allowed me to take the same class two years in a row. As a creative writing teacher, Mr. Chalmers helped me learn through his evaluations of my work. When I wrote a short story, he would give me straightforward feedback: "If you say your character's eyes are yellow, I assume he has jaundice. You need to make it clear that he has yellow eyes because he's from another planet." It was practical feedback. He gave my stories a second chance by letting me rewrite them. With his guidance, I was able to craft short stories that won writing awards.

I had learned from Mr. Chalmers because I had been willing to take his feedback and make it part of my work. Now I had an opportunity to do the same with my students' feedback. I resolved to incorporate their suggestions into my teaching methods.

Over the next few years, I made some important changes to my course and to my teaching. I stopped taking attendance. I let students know participation in class exercises was voluntary. I dropped exercises that students felt had little value, and adopted alternative exercises that they suggested. One of the most significant changes I made was to give students the option of rewriting and resubmitting their essays after I had graded them. (After all, what good did it do to return an essay covered with red ink if a student had no opportunity to do something with the feedback?)

Over the years, the evaluations of my Management Communications class steadily improved. I began seeing comments such as, "The instructor helped build confidence and self-esteem," "We laughed a lot while learning," and one I particularly enjoyed, "Tag is an excellent instructor. She should get a big wage increase!"

This spring, several years after my first student feedback, I opened my evaluations to find that I had scored 4.95 out of 5.0 on "Overall rating of instructor"—a 99% approval rating. Oh well, I thought with a smile, you can't please everyone.

TAG GOULET
Calgary, Canada

Exchange of Gifts

*L*IFE'S MOST IMPORTANT lessons come in the least expected ways and the most unusual packages. Throughout my twenty-five years of teaching I have witnessed students learn many such lessons, yet I never cease to be amazed and inspired each and every time it happens.

For eight years I coordinated a dropout recovery school. The school intentionally served students who were castoffs, throwaways, and underachievers of all types. I designed the school to demonstrate that every student was salvageable and that all it really took was an investment of time, love, caring, respect, and high expectations. My reputation as a classroom teacher was fun, yet tough. I expected everyone to work hard, and my students knew this. They also knew I really cared.

When I started the Independent Learning Center, I wanted students to see what important contributions they could actually make toward bettering themselves and their community. Along with the regular core curriculum and self-science courses there was a requirement to perform a minimum of sixty hours of community service. Most of my students had never been asked to give of themselves. Many, in fact, thought that they had nothing of value to give. Jason was one of those students.

Jason was a tall, strong, well-built, tough, seventeen-year-old former gang leader. After experiencing a variety of problems in school, he enrolled himself in the Independent Learning Center. The requirements were that he give up all gang activities, do a minimum of thirty hours of homework every week, and perform the sixty hours of community service. He agreed to the requirements, started in the program, and was actually doing a remarkable job of performing academically. Each week he brought in the sufficient requirement of high-quality homework. He and I had many discussions about his family, his past behaviors, how he became who he was, and even his dreams and aspirations for the future, in fact, he wasn't sure he had much of a future. I got to know him as a very bright, intelligent young man who always wore a mask of toughness. In spite of that, or maybe because of that, I grew very fond of Jason.

All was going well those first few months until I told him that it was time to begin his community service. His words to me were, "I'm not going to do that sh——." Patiently, I reminded him that he was required to do at least sixty hours of community service in order to remain enrolled in the school. If he chose not to do it, he would have to go to another school. He said it was the first time he had ever liked school and that if I were a good teacher, I would let him graduate without doing that "stupid stuff." I said, "Jason, the community service part of the requirement is not negotiable." He stared at me for a long time and finally said, "Fine, if I have to do it, just pick something; but I won't like it."

I hooked him up as a reader, with Bessie, a blind eighty-two-year-old woman who was in a local nursing home. When I brought Jason to meet Bessie, he brought along a somewhat sleazy (bordering on pornographic) novel. He told me that was what he would read to the "old bag."

After the introduction, I started to leave. As I walked out the door I heard Bessie say, quite emphatically, "That is not the book I want you to read." She pulled out a copy of Stephen Crane's, *The Red Badge of Courage* from under her pillow, and said, "Read this." Jason looked shocked, but reluctantly put his novel back into his pocket, took Bessie's book, and began to read. Quietly, I left the room, a knowing smile on my face.

Two hours later, Jason came back to the school. I asked him how things had gone with Bessie. He replied, "I'm not going back." When I asked him why, he said, "I'm just not!" Again, I reminded him about the requirements and said we would talk about it before the next reading date.

Several days later, just before he was scheduled to go back for his second session of reading, Jason came to me and again said, "Redenbach, I really do not want to go back there! The nursing home stinks, there are a bunch of old people wandering in and out, and I feel weird and out of place."

I responded, "Sometimes in life we have to push beyond our comfort zone and go beyond our own needs in order to serve others. This is one of those times, Jason. Go back just one more time and let me know how it turns out."

Later, when I saw Jason, I asked him how it went. Every time I remember his words, my throat tightens.

"As I walked to the door of her room," Jason said, "she must have recognized my footsteps. I stepped toward her, and I heard her say, 'Oh Jason. It's you! My eyes have come back to me.'" His voice cracked when he said, "I just stood there and felt the tears well up in my eyes. I guess she really needed me. No one has ever needed me before." Then quietly I heard him say, "I guess I'll keep going back. *The Red Badge of Courage* is a good book."

Jason continued to read to Bessie. They became good friends until Bessie died a few years later. Jason had given a special gift to Bessie—he had been her eyes, as well as her good friend. In return, Bessie gave Jason an equally special gift—the feeling that he was needed and the knowledge that he could make a positive difference in the life of another person. What a beautiful lesson to learn.

SANDI REDENBACH
Davis, California

Role Reversal

$\mathcal{A}$ WAVE OF self-pity was about to sweep over me when I heard a fairly loud voice say, "Hey, Mrs. B!"

I'd been left temporarily alone at the receptionist's window in the oncology/radiology department at St. John's Hospital, where I'd dutifully reported to consult with my doctor and schedule thirty-six radiation treatments for breast cancer.

I'd already gone through surgery and five of nine chemotherapy treatments. "What's next?" I thought with a sigh.

I turned around in the direction of the voice, expecting—however unlikely, given the circumstances—to see a former student. But I didn't recognize the young man.

"Who are you?" I asked, with a forced smile.

"You taught at Will Rogers School," the young man replied, "didn't you? Gordi Barba recognized you first. He was in your class. I'm Francisco de la Torre. I was never in your class, but you had all my brothers and sisters. Gordi and I are radiation therapists here."

It's easy to say that our students are our future. But it's another thing entirely to know that your future, if there is to be one, is now completely in their capable, caring hands.

I could hardly believe it. I'd been through so much already, and now I was going to have former students for my radiation therapists.

"Well," I laughed, "soon you'll be seeing a lot of me. And I mean that in every possible sense."

The young man laughed and returned to work. I opened my calendar, turned to the receptionist, and scheduled my thirty-six appointments.

As I wandered off to find my husband, I thought back to the meeting we'd had with the doctor earlier that morning. When he'd heard I was a teacher, he had spoken so respectfully and at such length about the importance of educators, about the widespread influence our work has on society at-large.

And here, right in his office, two students from the school where I'd taught second and third grade for eighteen years were radiation therapists. Can you believe that?

When I found my husband, I related the incident to him and we laughed. We tried to think of some funny one-liners I could slip into hospital conversations.

"How about, 'If I ever kept you in at recess to do your homework, now is the time to retaliate,'" I suggested.

Daily radiation for nearly two months allowed me to reestablish contact with these two fine young men. They told me how they'd gotten their radiation certificates in Utah while working in California. They told me about their families, activities with their children, and about their siblings' families and careers.

As they went about their important daily work, I felt privileged to observe how compassionately and professionally they treated all their patients.

What a pleasure it was for me to see Francisco play Santa Claus at the hospital Christmas party and to tell all who'd listen that he'd been a student at the school where I taught way back when.

What a surprise to see Gordi's mother again after so many years. I'd had so many parent-teacher conferences with her in the past, and now, as she accompanied a friend going through radiation, I had the chance to hear what had become of so many former students from her neighborhood.

What a delight to be surrounded by so many people connected to me by more than mere professional obligation.

What a blessing to remember my time in the "radiation chamber" fondly, to think of it as an upbeat leg of the journey to reclaim my health. The experience brought something full circle in my life as a teacher.

It's easy to say that our students are our future. But it's another thing entirely to know that your future, if there is to be one, is now completely in their capable, caring hands.

I know how lucky I am—to be alive and to be a teacher.

DIANE BRUNSON
Rancho Palos Verdes, California

I Touch the Future

$\mathcal{W}$HEN I WAS a high school student almost forty years ago, I had little tolerance for my old female teachers with their thick-soled shoes, bulging stomachs, sagging breasts, gray hair, and bifocals. I wondered why they didn't retire and give young teachers who I could relate to a chance to teach and make learning fun.

Now, more than three-and-a-half decades later and facing retirement, I've become the teacher I used to criticize and laugh at so very long ago. I wear cushiony Easy Spirit orthopedic shoes every working day. My stomach, breasts, and rear not only protrude, they droop. My gray hair demands brown dye every month. Like a '65 Mustang in for repairs, I was hospitalized twice last year, and I cope with bifocals.

What's forced me to face my own professional mortality is this year's batch of new teachers. I now realize how dated I've become. I still prefer whole-class instruction to groups. My classroom writing models come from literary classics instead of rap lyrics. I still grade papers with a red pen. I'm serious and content-oriented, not "fun." But I like to think that I'm a good mentor, that I grade fairly, and that most students appreciate my stern demeanor and realize it's my way of wanting them to take school as seriously as I believe it should be taken. I also believe that even though I've grown tired and old in their eyes, I still have contributions to make in the classroom and to their lives. I love introducing adolescents to good literature and observing their writing mature throughout the year. I delight in seeing a student's poem printed in a school publication or local newspaper. I get a charge watching an enraptured class stare open-mouthed at a student-made video. And I rejoice in reading a composition written by a trusting pupil who admits feeling abandoned and heartbroken the day no one wanted to sit with him at lunch.

I truly admire those who now begin their careers in education. Teachers are faced with ever-increasing incidents of violence and criticism for our students' high failure and drop-out rates and low test scores; but these same teachers face huge enrollments of special-needs students, youngsters who have been ignored, abandoned, and abused and still others who speak little or no English. These educators spend their own money on teaching supplies in spite of earning an average of $36,000 a year. They are faced with the mandate of incorporating service-learning experiences in their curricula, struggling with block-scheduling, ninety-minute classes, and pleas for year-round schooling all the while completing paperwork at home most nights and weekends. To describe the plight of today's teachers, this sign hangs in our faculty lounge:

> *If a doctor, lawyer, or dentist had 25 people in his office at one time, all of whom had different needs, and some of whom didn't want to be there and were causing trouble, and the doctor, lawyer, or dentist, without assistance, had to treat them all with professional excellence for ten months, then he might have some conception of the classroom teachers' job.*

I've lived with bell schedules, parent conferences, starting new school years in September and finishing old ones in June so long that I know no other life. Tenured teaching brings academic freedom to me so I can read for school and write for publication, two great loves in my life. Of course, teaching fifteen-year-olds to enjoy reading and writing as I do is a yearly challenge, and, admittedly, some school years are more successful than others. But I know that the day I leave teaching, I leave the vitality of youth and won't daily witness the joys of discovery I see in these teens as they experience new beginnings: passing their drivers' tests, falling in love, ordering class rings, making the honor roll, scoring a winning touchdown, attending homecoming and prom, signing each other's yearbooks, or walking proudly across the stage to receive that diploma and wave a last good-bye. Maybe I'm reliving my youth each year through these students, and that's what keeps me from changing the constant in my life—teaching.

I don't have the courage to count the numbers of classes taught, parent-conferences, papers graded, and chaperone duties, but I still keep an old copy of *Up the Down Staircase* by Bel Kaufman on my desk, which was the subject of my own college admissions essay that I wrote as a high school senior so many years ago. Now, it seems as trite and dated as my essay, but I keep the book because it was the first I read of real-life teaching episodes. However, my own experiences have been equally as colorful.

> *Maybe I'm reliving my youth each year through these students, and that's what keeps me from changing the constant in my life—teaching.*

Some noteworthy experiences are upbeat and lighthearted. Recently, I was both amused and humbled to read one student's end-of-the-year evaluation: "You would be a *great* teacher if only you would update your wardrobe." I was even more delighted by another student's reply to the question, "How could I improve my class for next year?" He wrote, "Do just what you did this year—give 'em hell!"

A more serious episode occurred recently. Before each holiday season, I assign students to write a tribute and letter of thanks to one or both of their parents. The completed paper is boxed and wrapped. Then, I ask parents to do likewise for their child and send it to me in a sealed envelope to be read by the student on the final day of class. It's a poignant moment for all of us, and it's an assignment I wish I had completed for my own parents before I lost them. But this year, the unexpected happened. I received this letter from a student's father upon my return from winter break.

> *Each day I witness the competence of my fellow teachers who are dedicated and excellent role models. They are like candles that light others while consuming themselves.*

Christopher's mother passed away unexpectedly in her sleep on Christmas Eve. Chris and I are obviously devastated by the loss of his mother and my wife of twenty-seven years. I would like to thank you in advance for taking into account his feelings during this most difficult time. The tribute that Chris wrote to his mom as your class assignment on December 21, just four days before her death, so moved her that she wrote a tribute back to him. At her funeral service this past Tuesday, the minister read both Chris' tribute to his mom and her tribute back to him. This was a very moving moment for me and I thank you for assigning this. Little did I know it would be needed so soon.

I READ IN the papers that of all the professions, teachers are considered the most moral, upright, and honest. I also read that, according to the Ad Council, fifty-seven percent of Americans cite teachers as contributing the most to society as opposed to the twenty-five percent who believe that the medical profession gives the most and only one percent who believe lawyers do. Each day I witness the competence of my fellow teachers who are dedicated and excellent role models. They are like candles that light others while consuming themselves. They are ignited by the curiosity of children, they like their subject matter and young people, and they know they make a difference in the lives of their students. Teaching is their mission, their calling, and like Christa McAuliffe, they can claim, "I touch the future; I teach."

But perhaps a college professor I had many years ago characterized our profession the best when he recommended it to me, and I think it's the reason I'm still teaching:

> Teaching is a good way to make a living. Not only does one enjoy the process itself (how lovely the sound of one's own voice), but it's like being a 'doorkeeper in the house of the Lord,' which is authoritatively stated to be better than sitting in the seats of the scornful.

KATHY MEGYERI
Sandy Spring, Maryland

Labor of Love

A COUPLE OF weeks ago a persistent sore throat sent me reluctantly to the doctor's office. As I sat impatiently in the reception area, awaiting the call of my name, I discerned that the room was full of chatting, soon-to-be mothers in various stages of pregnancy. Scanning a three-month-old copy of *Better Homes and Gardens,* I tried unsuccessfully to turn a deaf ear to their incessant litany of symptoms. As their voices droned on, however, I was suddenly struck by a revelation: Although I have never been pregnant, I too, have experienced the identical aches, joys, and anxieties: I am a teacher. To teach is to vicariously experience the pangs of pregnancy—a nine-month odyssey of child development.

As I entered school that sleepy September morning, the stark reality that I have begun the first month of my first trimester registers in my already queasy stomach. My body and mind grow fatigued, thinking of the physical and emotional demands that await me in the ensuing nine months ahead. However, in the span of a minute, I find my mood swinging from uneasy fear to eagerness and anticipation, confident that my students will revel in the heroic antics of Beowulf, and feel the anguish of Marc Antony. Now buoyant in the belief that I will be the great Mother of Knowledge, my students silently enter the classroom. As I gaze into each pair of eyes, eager to discern the first flickers of life, the unwelcome urgency again emerges—just forty-seven minutes more and I shall be able to dash to the bathroom once again. Thus September passes.

Although I have never been pregnant, I too, have experienced the identical aches, joys, and anxieties: I am a teacher. To teach is to vicariously experience the pangs of pregnancy—a nine-month odyssey of child development.

Although October and November carry with them many symptoms reminiscent of September, I find myself experiencing new and confusing ones as well. The fatigue and nausea still plague my days, but accompanying them now are irrational and unexplained cravings. I am suddenly filled with the desire to change my kitchen shelf paper or clean those long forgotten closets, chores that would have never entered my mind during those carefree, pre-contract months. However, now that I am held captive in my new surroundings, the cravings intensify. The days are marked by occasional headaches; my body is still adjusting to the enormity of the task that lies ahead. Thinking I now detect movement and life within my students, my hopes are dashed: Movement will not occur until the fourth month—closer to report card day. As November emerges, my mood swings occur with less frequency, and I now experience a welcome sense of calmness; Thanksgiving vacation is near.

With fatigue still its vanguard, the second trimester of child development begins. The annoying mild swelling in my ankles and feet, though unwelcome, is now expected, as is the nagging backache; all painful reminders of the seven hours spent daily on my feet explaining the difference between metaphors and similes. Nasal congestion now begins to plague me; after all, December is the breeding ground of virus-infected children, as yet unschooled in the art of covering one's mouth during a sneezing attack. Although my mood swings have temporarily stabilized, I discover that irritability is now second nature to me; consistently late assignments and bickering children are beginning to erode my normally pleasing personality. (Although the bickering *does* at least indicate movement and life!)

January and February, too, are unkind in their contributions to my delicate condition. My clothes, now too snug from the months of faculty lounge doughnuts and potato chips, are relegated to the back of closet as new and unfashionable "fat" clothes replace them. Unpredictable anxiety attacks intermittently appear and disappear with staggering speed—fears that my weight gain will be permanent or my students are not progressing as they should. However, as February draws to a close, my anxiety is replaced with a new, and often, frightening boredom with my condition. The novelty and excitement of my odyssey has waned, and I resign myself to my fate.

Since March has arrived like a lamb, I steel myself for my final trimester, aware that the inevitable lion awaits me. My students are now extremely active, allowing me no peace during the day. The difficulty I experience sleeping nights is evident as I force my swelling, cramping legs to drag me around the room for individual student conferences; after all, the welfare of my students is my main concern. As my temples pound, my feelings of boredom begin to dissipate, replaced by an uneasy apprehension. In less than three months my students will be released into the world, and it is my responsibility to prepare them! Calming myself with the knowledge that the end is near, I painfully continue my rounds. The hemorrhoids are not improving; the continuous strain of the weight of my students assaults my body. Two more months and this torture will end.

April and May differ little from the aches and pains of March, yet now it is my emotional state that dominates my thinking. Still anxious and impatient, I daydream and fantasize about the fate of my students, visualizing that Joel will win his scholarship and Susie will be accepted by her dream college in the East. Lost in the revelry of my fantasies, I am seized by a crippling pain; final exams are complete and the task of grading them awaits—my labor has begun. With measured breaths and an eye on the clock, I struggle to deliver final grades to the office. Urged on by the support of fellow teachers who assure me that I am doing fine, it is time to push; grades are due in less than fifteen minutes! Exhausted, I summon my last ounce of strength and record the final score. With a giddy sense of relief and tenderness, I cradle the grade sheets in my arms. It is over. I have succeeded. I have given birth to a new class of graduates.

As the relatives gather, the flashes of Polaroid cameras record the miracle. All memories of pain and anxiety fade as I feel the touch of my students shaking my hands or hugging me in tearful good-byes, with diplomas clutched tightly to their breasts. These are my children, they are products of nine months of my love and nurturing. While I watch my fledglings reach out to the world, thoughts of new children enter my mind. Forgetting the trials and tribulations I will experience, I turn my eye to the future, and prepare for the conception of the next class. I do hope to have an easier time next year.

NANCY SAMP
El Dorado, Kansas

Big Guy

*T*HE SCHOOL YEAR started just like all the others. I received my new sixth graders and began the process of getting to know them. It didn't take long due to the fact that this was a small class of youngsters with learning disabilities. I took special notice of a particular young man as he entered the classroom. Jeff was so tall that he couldn't fit into any of our elementary-sized desks. I soon found myself referring to him as "Big Guy."

As days progressed into weeks, I discovered that Jeff was an angry young man with a terrible temper. He would get mad, throw a tantrum, and jolt out of the classroom on a regular basis. It was clear that my primary task was to teach him to control his rage. He and I spent many hours those first few weeks discussing anger-management strategies. At first, I couldn't tell if it was making any difference, until one day while I was lecturing him about not turning in math homework. Jeff stood up and left the room, however this time he did not throw a tantrum. I searched the hallways for him, but he was nowhere to be found. Later, as I walked to the phone to call the office about his whereabouts, I noticed him standing at the door watching me.

"Why did you walk out, Jeff?"

"I was losing it, but I didn't want to yell at you," he replied.

That brief conversation indicated that an important bridge had been built between us.

As the year progressed, things continued to improve for Jeff. There was a dramatic shift in his behavior at school; he was participating in school sports activities, developing friendships with the other students, and improving his grades. Granted, Jeff still had a few problems to resolve, but overall, he and I were pleased with the emotional and behavioral changes that were taking place.

The following school year, Jeff was once again assigned to my classroom. One morning early in the year, he limped into my math class and asked if he could use a chair to prop up his leg. He explained that he had hurt his knee the day before and his mom was picking him up after lunch to take him to the doctor. Although I would ordinarily decline such a request, I said, "Yes, prop up your knee." I didn't realize at the time that God was guiding me, sparing me insurmountable guilt in days to come.

The following Monday morning I was standing in the hallway outside of my homeroom, when a group of students approached me with words that struck my heart like lightning.

"Mrs. Ross, did you hear about Jeff? He has cancer in his knee."

Traumatized by the news that Jeff had cancer, I struggled to make it through school that day.

Jeff returned to school several days later. I arranged for the other students to go to the library, so I could have a private chat with him. I have never been more proud of anyone than I was of Jeff that day. He smiled his angelic, silly smile and told me not to worry, that he would be fine.

But worry I did. Jeff underwent one operation after another to fight the reoccurring tumors that doctors found in his body. He came to school from time to time, but spent much of his school year in the hospital undergoing chemotherapy and various treatments that we all hoped would put his cancer in remission.

Our school sponsored several events on his behalf. We purchased video games to help him pass the time in the hospital. Because he had missed picture day, the entire eighth grade decided to make a special one for him. The students wore red and white clothing and stood in formation spelling out the word, *Hi*. Our art teacher took the photo, had it enlarged, and then delivered it to Jeff's hospital room. He proudly displayed the poster-sized photo above his hospital bed. When Jeff returned home, our local video store provided free movies and video game rentals. Our school community also raised thousands of dollars in donations to assist the family with Jeff's medical expenses. It was indeed heartwarming to see an entire school taking special care of one of their students.

Then in January of that year, Jeff's mother asked me if I would tutor him at home. She had contacted the school administration and they had given their approval. Of course, I said "yes" and began working with him on a weekly basis. Some weeks were missed when he was undergoing painful treatments. Sometimes I found it difficult persuading him to work on mundane learning tasks when he was fighting for his life.

The kids at school stayed in touch with Jeff and did not see him as "the learning-disabled kid with cancer." Instead they admired and respected his courageous battle.

Jeff started his freshman year of high school with his peers. He struggled to keep up with his academic program, sometimes missing school because of doctor's appointments and treatments. I was no longer tutoring him at home, but I still called or visited weekly. I had grown to love this now six-foot-seven "Big Guy." He was like a son to me.

As weeks turned into months, in spite of his valiant battle, it appeared that Jeff was losing the war. His cancer kept reoccurring and, at this point, it was evident that he had made a decision to stop fighting.

I continued to visit him on a regular basis, listening attentively as he shared humorous stories about his life. I cherish the intimate conversations we had during that time. Then one cloudy November day, I received an urgent call from Jeff's mother.

"I think you should come to see him soon," she said as her voice wavered. I drove to Jeff's house right after school, and spent a couple of hours chatting with him. He told me stories that had me giggling and laughing so hard, tears were rolling down my face. Some of his friends from school also dropped by while I was there, and we all had a wonderful visit.

When it was time to go, I gently patted him on the shoulder and said, "See ya, Big Guy." Although his usual reply was, "Later," this time, he looked up, grabbed my hand, held it, smiled, and said, "Bye!"

Instinctively, I knew he was telling me the end was near. I felt a deep sense of love and sadness, but held back the sobs that would come later.

Jeff died the next day.

His mother and father asked me to give the eulogy at his funeral. His dad insisted that I tell lighthearted and humorous stories about Jeff. I was terrified, but I knew I had to do this one last thing for Jeff and his family. I worked on my speech for hours.

When I arrived at the funeral home a few days later, I was escorted to the front of the room. I looked out over the podium and took in the hundreds and hundreds of faces, young and old, that had come to say their final good-byes to Jeff. I swallowed hard and delivered the speech that I believed he would have loved. I spoke from my heart, rather than my notes. I had them laughing, as Jeff's dad had requested, but we were also crying.

Looking back, I can say without hesitation that the day of Jeff's funeral was the saddest day of my life. This six-foot-seven young man taught me about living and dying courageously. I believe that God put me on this earth to serve kids like Jeff. Although Jeff may be gone, he will never be forgotten. It was an honor to be part of his life.

EDIE ROSS
Danville, Indiana

Full Circle

*W*HEN I WAS in the third grade I wanted to be just like Mrs. Abshere. She had a Dorothy Hamill haircut, wore high heels, and always had a smile for her students. She took extra time to go over math concepts with me or praise my poetry. She rarely raised her voice and was respected by every one of her students. She made us feel both special and wanted. During recess, I would stay inside and play school, and Mrs. Abshere would lovingly let me use her special pens and worksheets. "You're a good teacher, Erin," she would say.

I was considered a "high-risk" child. My family had little money and my mother's abusive boyfriend lived in our home. One of the reasons that I loved school was because it provided an escape, and I truly felt that Mrs. Abshere cared about me. Her patience and kindness helped me through many hard times. She used to carry a little tube of lip gloss and offer me some during story time. "Chapped lips hurt and we must take care of them," she'd say. I thought of her somewhat like a surrogate mom and a model of the kind of person I hoped to be someday.

One day, after my mother had been involved in welfare fraud, the police came and arrested her. I was nine years old and scared to death! I held onto my brother and sister as we were driven to a children's home.

As my mother awaited her sentence, my brother, sister, and I waited in the children's home. We went to a school provided by the home and slept in a room filled with other children whose parents were also in custody. Soon days turned into weeks and I wondered if we would ever return to our parents. When I was told that my mother would be serving a six-month sentence, my hopes dwindled. The state was unable to locate my natural father, so in a few months, arrangements would be made for adoption.

As I walked back to my bunk, I felt numb. I was no longer nine years old writing poetry and playing school. I was now a prisoner and didn't understand why. I fell on my bed and sobbed for hours. I was mad at the world and no longer saw any future for myself. It was while I was in this state of mind that one of the girls came running up to me. "Hey, there's a lady here to see you. I think it's your mom." A flood of emotion came over me as I ran down the hall. *Could it be true? Did they let her go?*

When I got to the end of the hallway, there stood the pretty lady with the Dorothy Hamill haircut. It was Mrs. Abshere! She held her arms out to me, "I know no one is better than your mom, honey, but I love you, too!" I hugged her and silently thanked God for bringing this angel thirty miles out of her way to see me.

After my hug, she reached in her pocket and took out the familiar lip gloss. "You still have chapped lips, I see." As I walked Mrs. Abshere around the grounds, I began to feel hopeful again. I showed her my bunk and a few poems I had written. I was so excited to show her off to all my new friends. "This is my teacher, Mrs. Abshere!" I yelled. I wanted everyone to know her name.

When our visit came to an end, Mrs. Abshere made me promise to come to school and say good-bye so she would know that I was okay. I promised.

I didn't know what would become of me. I only knew that I would survive—I would be okay—because a special teacher had shown that she cared.

Two weeks later, my grandparents were awarded custody of us. We would be moving across the state. My grandma drove me to school so I could say good-bye to all my friends. When it came time to say good-bye to Mrs. Abshere, I just couldn't do it. I stood there and tried not to look at her. Sadness overwhelmed me; how could I leave this wonderful woman? As I stood there, tears streaming down my cheeks, she handed me a box and said, "This is a box filled with special teacher pens and worksheets so you can play school whenever you like. Every time you play, I hope you'll think of

FULL CIRCLE

me because I will be thinking of you." I will never forget those words.

As my grandma and I drove off, I didn't know what would become of me. I only knew that I would survive—I would be okay—because a special teacher had shown that she cared. That knowledge was enough to get me through anything.

Sixteen years later, I searched for Mrs. Abshere so I could tell her how grateful I was. When I found her, we had the most wonderful conversation. I felt so much pride telling her that I was only a year away from becoming a teacher myself. "Oh!" she exclaimed, "You can student teach in my room!" So, perhaps I will be returning to Mrs. Abshere's classroom soon, only this time, as a peer and a very grateful friend.

ERIN KELLEY
Antioch, California

I Knew He Could Do It!

*T*HERE WERE SO many children that touched my life during my years spent teaching, but as the years continue to pass, thoughts of one young man have crossed my mind more frequently than others. His name is Marcos.

At the time I met him, I taught fifth grade in an area predominantly populated by U.S. immigrants who worked in the fields surrounding the area. As usual I began my year by asking the children how many of them intended on graduating from high school. Then I asked who planned on earning a college degree. Much to my dismay very few children raised their hands in response to my first question, and even fewer responded to my second question. I spent much of my time encouraging the children to continue their schooling. We discussed the benefits of having an education, and I helped them set goals toward achieving their high school diplomas. To most of these children, an education was something that seemed beyond their reach. Marcos was different.

He was a precious child, always smiling, witty, and full of life. I can honestly say that I was always happy to see him. Marcos frequently asked me if I believed he would leave the barrio where he lived and whether I believed he could really make it through school and beyond. As always, I'd respond with positive words of encouragement, telling him that I absolutely knew he would do it. I knew he would not only graduate from high school, but that he'd continue to succeed from there in whatever area he chose to pursue.

When our time together was ending, Marcos and I said our good-byes. We'd been through so much together in a year's time, and had become much like a family. I loved and respected each and every one of my students, and Marcos was no exception. I asked him to please keep in contact with me. I wanted to know about his successes and share in his happiness, as well as help him any way I could.

The years passed, and soon I was transferred to another school district. One day, as I was finishing up my lessons with another class of children, in walked a young man. I watched him enter my classroom, unsure at first as to who he was. But, as soon as he smiled, it was clear to me who I was looking at. It was Marcos, and he was waving his very first paycheck at me. "I've been looking all over for you!" he said. "I wanted to show you my first paycheck and let you know that I'm really doing it! I'm succeeding!" I could see the confidence in his eyes.

Given the area in which he had grown up, he had indeed beaten the odds—he had a job and was now earning a steady income. I was thrilled to introduce this young man to my class and allow the students to congratulate him on his achievement.

After I dismissed my class, Marcos and I continued to visit for some time getting caught up on the previous five years and talking about some of the other children he and I knew. I grieved to hear about the ones who hadn't done as well, and was pleased to learn that some were succeeding just as Marcos was. When we parted, Marcos left me with promises of more successes and I left him with more words of confidence just as I had before.

Two more years passed and, again at the end of a very long day, I received word from Marcos. This time in the form of an envelope left in my mailbox at school. I opened the envelope to find a high school graduation announcement from Marcos. His picture fell out onto my desk, and as I picked it up I saw a handsome young man in a blue suit wearing a tie and a beautiful smile. It was my Marcos. Tears fell easily as I read of his latest accomplishments and his request for my presence at his graduation. I took the card home to share with my family. My husband, Stan sensed the pride and joy I felt for my former student's achievements, and he encouraged me to contact Marcos and tell him how I felt.

Contacting Marcos wasn't as easy as I had thought it would be. A return address wasn't on the announcement, so one night after our smaller children were tucked into bed, we left our older children in charge, and Stan and I drove to the area where I had taught so many years before. As we walked up to the small and crowded house, we could hear many voices, most of them children. There must have been over twenty people in the tiny home. We could see them as we knocked on the door and watched through the hole where a door knob had once been. A young man answered our knock. Stan spoke better Spanish, so he asked for Marcos. He explained that I had once been his teacher and that I wanted to give him a gift. The young man explained to my husband that Marcos didn't live in the area anymore and he wasn't sure where he had moved.

Disappointed, we walked to our car and drove home. When I returned to work the next day I spent some time contacting individuals who could help me locate Marcos. By the end of the day I had an address. I drove to the address and was quite pleased to see that Marcos now lived in a better neighborhood. I walked up to the door and knocked. This time a woman answered. I quickly recognized her as Marcos' mother; she had the same warm smile. I explained to her, in my poor Spanish, that I was looking for Marcos. I had been one of his teachers and wanted to congratulate him on his graduation and give him a gift. She started telling me about all the wonderful changes Marcos had brought to their lives. He had a job after school and on the weekends. He'd worked hard to help earn enough money for he and his mother to move from the barrio to the home they were currently renting. She was so proud of him. "My Marcos," she said, proudly, "is a good boy." A good boy, yes, I thought to myself and on his way to being a great man.

Marcos wasn't there that day for me to see. I left my message and gift with his mother because I wouldn't be able to attend his graduation ceremonies. As I walked back to my car and drove the distance to my home, my heart was filled with gratitude for having had the opportunity to witness so much success in a child.

I have Marcos' picture on my refrigerator still to this day to serve as a reminder to me as to why I choose to teach. It's been four years since I heard from him last, but I look forward to celebrating the next message of success with him. Charles Dickens once said of children, "It's a privilege and an honor to be in the presence of them who have so recently dwelt with God." He was right.

JULIE STEINEPREIS
Higley, Arizona

Back to School

*A*N INFLUENTIAL TEACHER is not always one we've had in elementary school or high school. Some great teachers show up later in our lives, perhaps in the midst of a crisis. Dr. Memo Mendez, a professor at National University was that person in my life.

Not very long ago, I was sitting in a divorce attorney's office at the age of fifty, in the process of ending a twenty-six year marriage. I had a ten year old, a twelve year old, and a pregnant seventeen-year-old daughter. After my husband left, I got my very first job, earning a mere eight dollars and fifty cents an hour. It was August. My daughter's baby was due in October. Because I already had a four-year college degree, my attorney advised that I go back to school for a teaching credential.

My life was a mess! I had to sell the house, find a new place to live (with three kids, a baby, and a dog), try to keep up with the bills, and work overtime while preparing for a new grand-child. Hoping to earn a decent living while doing something I knew I'd love, I took my attorney's advice and signed up for school that September.

Classes were held two nights a week from five thirty to ten in the evening. On the first day of school, I went to Room 101 for Curriculum and Instruction. It had been thirty years since I'd been in a classroom. Anxious thoughts raced through my mind as I sat at a desk waiting for the class to begin.

Then Dr. Mendez appeared and began to speak. He painted a glorious picture of teaching, and it wasn't long before I found myself engaged and enthused about this new learning process; my black-and-white world was suddenly becoming colorful again.

There were twelve of us in Dr. Mendez's class. He expected us to collaborate on class projects. He provided us with opportunities to work in groups and to contribute our strengths to each other. His assignments were challenging and exciting!

Dr. Mendez taught us how to prepare a lesson and then requested that we take turns teaching lessons to the class. We shared our ideas and provided positive feedback to one another. We were not allowed to be negative or critical. Dr. Mendez rarely criticized; but concentrated on the positive aspects of our work and effort.

Some nights I went to class with tears running down my face; my emotions in turmoil, my body tired from a fifty-hour work week. My fellow students and I bonded. They provided me with a much needed support system and often offered encouragement in the form of jokes, Kleenex, and compelling motivational lectures.

When Dr. Mendez taught, time flew. I couldn't believe how much fun it was to learn in his class. I felt my mind opening up; I regained my enthusiasm for living. Dr. Mendez provided me with hope for the future: "You can do it," he proclaimed, and I believed him. "Yes, I can be a teacher!" "Yes, I can support my family!" "Yes, I can survive the divorce!" So, nose to the grindstone, I vowed to be the great teacher he described and modeled in his classroom.

Did I make it? Yes. I am proud to acknowledge that I am now an elementary teacher because Dr. Mendez showed me it was possible. What precious gifts he gave, not just to me, but to all the students I will serve in the coming years. I will bring Dr. Mendez's enthusiasm and optimism to my classroom. I will bring his love of learning, as well.

Yes, Dr. Mendez, I will pass on your gifts. Thank you for believing in me.

LEAH BECKS
San Bernardino, California

Perils of a
Preschool Husband

$\mathcal{M}$Y BELOVED AND I were zipping along about ten miles above the speed limit, two hundred miles north of San Francisco. Behind us, Andrew, our college sophomore, ahead of us, six hundred miles of the dullest driving west of Kansas, and then, home.

It was just before nine in the morning and my not yet caffeinated eyes were fighting the tourist-torpor brought on by four days of Andrew's excited shouts, "Hey, look at this! Ever see anything like that before?" Our twenty year old was proudly guiding us through the verdant splendor of the astonishing redwoods of Northern California's Humboldt County.

To my right, Jan, my wife was enjoying one of those, "You start the driving, I'll catch a snooze until you get tired," naps. Suddenly, I heard an anxious, imperative voice, punctuated by a piercing elbow to the ribs, "Oh, look. Stop!" Three thoughts overloaded my brain in the same millisecond that I floored the brakes and slid toward the road's shoulder. "What did I hit?" "Are you all right?" "What did we forget?" It was nothing of the sort. She pointed to the sawmill across the road and the piles of redwood sawdust—sawdust that would go great in the pouring table of her home away from home, Room 2 at the Growing Place Preschool.

Five minutes later we had made an illegal U-turn through the weeds of the road divider; made a deal to buy some sawdust from a guy who never quite understood what we were all about; stripped the pillow cases off the two pillows in the car to carry the damp chips home, and slathered through the beginnings of yet another rain shower to scoop soggy sawdust into the never-to-be-used-again pillow cases.

My wife, beatifically smiling, said, "The kids will love it." That single thought made the slipping, sliding, and purging of slimy sawdust out of her shoes worthwhile for her. Her smile made it worthwhile for me. You accept the inexplicable when you're married to a preschool teacher.

It isn't the sort of thing that you expect when you propose to a beautiful girl who had majored in dance education and went on to be a Radio City Music Hall Rockette. When our son Andrew turned three, we enrolled him at the Growing Place Preschool. Jan started working at the school as an assistant teacher. Andrew enjoyed preschool, and my wife found a new career.

The die was cast on the afternoon when she came home and said, "I think I'd like to keep teaching preschool after Andrew moves on. It'll keep me young." That was nineteen years ago. She still loves it, and without question, it has kept her young!

As a writer, I have written and produced over one hundred children's records, written for two honored children's television series, and created or co-created three network children's series. One would expect that I know a lot about kids. And I do. However, I've learned more about young children by sharing my life with a teacher who cares about the kids in her class just as if they were her own. She worries about their welfare both in and out of school. So, for all practical (and many impractical) purposes, her three- and four-year-old tikes become our extended family.

As our son moved on through schools and life, Jan's classes gave us other kids to laugh with and care for. Jan's school is not a day-care center, but rather a school where the entire staff is truly involved in the program and the children, collectively and individually. It's a requirement.

I know this because for nineteen years now, I've heard about what Sarah said, Peter did, Jennifer painted, and what Jason A. and Jason W. accomplished. I've heard about Melinda's improvements and Jake's shenanigans in the play yard. I've heard seemingly endless phone calls between Jan and other teachers as they tried to solve a child's problem; to reach over the horizon to find some new way to help.

Nineteen years of this and, for some reason, I love it more than ever. I know that I must be part of an army of men who never go into a store without keeping an eye open for stuff that might be useful to their preschool-teacher wives.

"Wow! Dinosaur shaped sponges. . . . I'll get six packages."
"Smelly markers at three bucks a pack; I wonder if three will be enough?" Every trip, to any kind of store, has the additional enticement of knowing that I might stumble onto something that we've never thought of before and that the kids would love. Guys who aren't married to preschool teachers never know the delight of holding up a package of wooden clothespins in all colors of the rainbow and saying hopefully, "Whaddayuh think? Only a buck and a half for twenty-eight of them." Then the joy of success that comes with the magic reply, "Great! I love 'em. Can you get six more?"

Guys who aren't married to preschool teachers never know the delight of holding up a package of wooden clothespins in all colors of the rainbow and saying hopefully, "Whaddayuh think? Only a buck and a half for twenty-eight of them."

A man who isn't married to a preschool teacher can't comprehend the magic moments as she tosses out ideas of how best to use his latest shopping discovery. "I wonder what we could do with those pins in the pouring table?" "With play-dough?" "Maybe if we glued two together?" It's a whole new area in which a husband can be creative and, as a bonus, keep his mind young and active.

Jan's preschool accepts children with special needs and there have been a scattering of autistic students. And attention deficit disorder? Where was it or what was it called when I was in school? She brings home the problems of these special students, their hopes, and their accomplishments and we've shared all these things together. Nowadays dinner table conversation at our place might focus on the autism or A.D.D. article we saw in Sunday's paper.

Jan's concerns about her students have become part of our lives. As a result, our life together has been richer and more fulfilled. Jan's career as a preschool teacher has given us an expansive vista of shared joys, accomplishments, and memories. Especially rewarding is the prospect that in spite of my getting ever older, each September I can look forward to a new group of names, faces, and personalities to hear about, laugh at, and love—Jan's classes, our extended family.

I would never have experienced that joy if my beloved hadn't thrown away the tap shoes and picked up the flannel board. As a job, it doesn't pay as much. As a life, the riches are unparalleled.

ROY FREEMAN
Thousand Oaks, California

A Lesson in Lipstick

I NEVER LIKED lipstick. At least, I didn't like when it created problems in my junior high school art class. I teach drawing to inner-city kids. Drawing requires a pencil, not a lipstick.

Carla and Zena, two young girls in my third period, were learning to negotiate the strange new territory of developing femininity. They became obsessed with what they found in their little mirrored compacts and adding lipstick to the equation further deepened their distraction from classwork. The next step: full-scale dependency on makeup and zero interest in schoolwork.

I was convinced that getting these two young ladies to abandon their lipstick would require the patience of Job. My name is Antonio, and waiting patiently for students to begin their work was not my strong suit.

Each day, during third period, Carla and Zena appeared to be preparing for a beauty pageant that I assumed was held during period four. The total output of their artwork occurred not in their drawing books, but on their faces. I reminded them on a daily basis, that the class assignments were an important part of their grade. It made little difference to them.

Each class period, as was my custom, I walked around the room helping students. One day, I was surprised to see that the girls appeared to be doing classwork. Twenty minutes later, however, approaching the rear of the classroom where the two girls sat, I noticed a mirror propped up underneath the desk on Carla's lap. I realized I had been snookered. My two young beauty contestants had continued with their cosmetology. I slipped up behind them. Then, with the laser-like accuracy of a well-planned surgical air strike, I swooped down, scooping up all their beauty products with both hands. I piled the whole affair atop my desk and told the girls they could collect everything after class on the proviso they keep it out of my classroom. I was relieved that we had resolved this interruption and happily returned to helping students.

Little did I suspect that this was just Act One in an episodic ritual that continued for days and weeks. As the semester progressed, their makeup became more sophisticated and involved. Tweezers busily plucked at their eyebrows, lids became overburdened with darker hues, and pancake lived up to its name. As the makeup grew heavier their artwork grew lighter—as in less and less.

Troubled by their growing disinterest in my drawing lessons, I wondered what I could do to change the devolving dynamic. Each day they came armed with new lipstick and other beauty products. Each day I would confiscate them. I no longer returned things at the end of the period. Instead, I promised they could have the contraband at the end of the semester or whenever their parents made time to meet with me.

Carla claimed I abridged her constitutional rights necessary to help students learn. Perhaps I had, but I was desperate to get her focused on artwork. She knew she was not skilled enough to argue law or logic, and we both knew that she had no business doing her makeup in class. We'd reached a stalemate.

I decided from the onset that the problem with Carla and Zena would be mine alone. It was not something to refer to the principal. I had to find a fair and equitable solution without resorting to a higher authority. But what? How? I was at my wits end and losing patience with each passing day. My normally upbeat demeanor was eroding, and I began snapping at students during period three. I developed a growing dislike for the two girls and eventually for my whole third period class. It was obviously time to take stronger measures. Utilizing the power granted to teachers over students, I issued detentions and threatened suspensions if they continued with their beauty work. Zena, fearful of parental consequences stopped. Carla continued, directly challenging me to a test of wills.

Carla's eyes now cut me with every glance. It was awful. I called her home to arrange a parent conference only to find a disconnected telephone. The next day I threatened to send Carla to the principal if I didn't hear from her parents by the end of the week. With hatred in her eyes, she informed me, "My mother works two jobs, and my father's dead!"

Her words took the breath from my body and gripped my heart. I left school that day numbed by thoughts of Carla not having a father. I was profoundly sorry for not being more caring and sensitive to her needs. It was shortly thereafter that I entered a space of internal inquiry, examining my role in this whole lipstick affair. I was able to see how important it was to consider my behavior and shortcomings when dealing with problems in the classroom. I realized that teachers often acknowledge only the student's role and responsibility when dealing with classroom issues.

The following Saturday, while driving my daughter Marissa and her friend Meredith to Golden Gate Park, I discovered a solution to my dilemma. The back seat of my old Plymouth was filled with joyous laughter. I looked into the rear view mirror and found the two young girls painting their faces with makeup. I was smiling as I watched them trying to adhere long eyelashes to heavily shadowed eyelids. I laughed out loud as they attempted to apply lipstick while in a moving car. Clearly neatness was not a priority.

While enjoying the scene in the rear view mirror, I reflected back to my classroom. I envisioned the scowl I wore admonishing Carla for using makeup in my art class. Suddenly, I realized how wrong I had been to dichotomize the feelings I had about my daughter and my student. The distinction revealed a gaping hole in my heart. I loved Marissa and her friend, but my caring for Carla and my other students was conspicuous only by its absence. It was painful to acknowledge all the years I had been teaching without love and compassion. I was relieved when we finally arrived in Golden Gate Park, as my vision had begun to blur from the tears in my eyes.

That weekend, I bought a full length mirror. It was a nice one, with a curved top and bevel around the edge. I brought it to school on Monday, arriving a bit earlier than usual. I needed some extra time before class started to begin working on my redemption. I opened my supply closet searching for just the right colors. Then, with a special lettering brush painted bright acrylic letters across the top of the mirror, following the beveled curve. I secured the mirror to the front wall of the classroom, right next to the pencil sharpener, and finished just as the bell sounded for first period. I couldn't wait for third period to begin. I didn't know what I would say or do, but I knew I wanted to make amends to Carla.

At the beginning of period three I announced to Carla that I had something important to tell her. She eyed me suspiciously. Slowly, I recounted my epiphany, my realization that I had been teaching without love. Carla, somewhat softened but still a little wary, waited to hear what else I had to say. I told her that from that moment on she could use the mirror for her beauty work. "Furthermore," I said, "if you would like to use a bigger mirror, you may use this one." With a sweep of my arm I tore down the butcher paper that covered the mirror. The classroom vibrated with a cheer let loose by the students. I invited Carla up to see the inscription across the top. Aloud, she read to the class "The Carla Garcia Memorial Mirror." When she read the inscription, she shouted, "I'm not dead, yet, Mr. Strano!"

"No, of course not," I replied. But this mirror is to remind me to always teach with an open heart."

Period three Art soon became my favorite class. The atmosphere was lighter and more enjoyable for everyone, but especially for Carla and me. Carla made good use of her new mirror, but within days she turned her attention to classwork and in fact became quite skilled at drawing. She often requested my personal attention to help her with her artwork, and she even relinquished her sneer for a perpetual smile. Where her face had seemed dark, it was now radiant. Where her personality had been angry, it was now joyous. I was so happy at the complete turn of events that I sorely missed her presence in class when she failed to show up for an entire week. I wondered what happened to her.

The following Monday she appeared at my classroom door. One eye was black and blue and both lips were swollen. A deep red bruise accentuated her high cheekbone. I immediately approached her and asked what had happened. Her swollen jaw could barely form words. With much coaxing she said she'd tell what happened but only if I promised not to repeat what she was about to tell me. I agreed. Slowly, struggling, fighting back tears and forcing whispers through her teeth, she told me her mother had beaten her. I was stunned! I told her that her mother was not allowed to beat her and that an agency called Child Protective Services was available to provide counseling for parents who hit their kids. Of course, Carla begged me not to submit a report because, she said, "my mother will kill me." I promised her that the agency would protect her from these kinds of things ever happening again. I begged her to trust and believe in me. Slowly, after many reassuring words, I convinced her to let me contact CPS. At last, she agreed. I escorted her to the vice-principal's office where we made the call that changed her life. I reassured her that things would be fine and left her with the vice-principal, awaiting the CPS officer.

It was another full week before I saw Carla again. She came running into my room at the start of period three. Traces of her beating were still apparent but all the swellings had subsided and the bruises were fading. She smiled and yelled, "Mr. Strano, Mr. Strano, my father is alive, my father is alive!" *How could that be?* I wondered. She explained, "When I was a little girl my mother told me that my father was dead. When we had the meeting with CPS they asked where my father was. I told them he was dead, but then my mother admitted he was really alive somewhere in Northern California! CPS found him and arranged a meeting." Over the next few weeks, Carla had a number of visits with her father who was living in a residential facility north of San Francisco.

In the afterglow of the events that occurred those few weeks, I was lulled into imagining a long and happy friendship with Carla. It came as a shock when Carla came to class one day to collect her artwork. Her mother was moving outside of the school district, and she would be transferring to a new school. Carla seemed to have mixed emotions as she gathered all her materials, came up to the front of the room, and gave me a big hug. She said she wanted to take the Carla Garcia Memorial Mirror with her, but thought the other students (who periodically used the mirror) would miss it; she was leaving it to my third period class.

With a quiver in her voice she said, "Thanks for everything you taught me Mr. Strano."

"No, Carla," I replied. "Thank *you* for all that you taught *me*." She walked out of the class quickly and I assumed I would never see her again. I was grateful to have known her and been her teacher.

The following September, not long after I had explained to my new art students why I had a Carla Garcia Memorial Mirror attached to the wall, Carla strolled into my classroom. I was amazed at how much she had grown up during the past six months. She had turned the corner from adolescent girl to beautiful young lady.

Although she looked different, she still had her familiar laugh and peppery language as she shared her version of how the Carla Garcia Memorial Mirror found its way into my classroom. Leaving out the personal details, she told only the funny things and had me laughing along with the students. The class applauded as she finished her story, and we all said good-bye and wished her well.

As my students returned to their artwork, my thoughts lingered on my journey with Carla. We had faced some very hard times early in the school year. However, even though we'd had our difficulties, our struggle ultimately brought us unexpected gifts. Through compassion and love, Carla built a new relationship with her mother and father, and I found my path as a teacher.

ANTONIO STRANO
Sausalito, California

The Student Teacher

*E*ARLIER THIS YEAR, I gave my fourth-grade class an unusual math assignment. They were to spend one thousand dollars on anything they wanted. "Purchases" were made by flipping through magazines, newspapers, catalogs, and so forth and clipping out items to put in a report. The total amount, including shipping and tax was to be exactly one thousand dollars, not a penny more, not a penny less.

Jacob, one of my ten-year-old boys was less academically gifted than the others and had recently been diagnosed with Tourette's syndrome, a genetic condition that causes "tics" or sudden uncontrollable movements and sounds, often during times of stress. What could be more stressful than delivering a report in front of your peers?

While Jacob was delivering his message, his tics surfaced and he had to control the jerking of his arm and leg, as well as the twitching of his mouth and neck. For a moment, I felt uncomfortable; I didn't want the students jeering at him. But, as I looked around the room, I noticed the students listening intently to Jacob's report. They were aware of his physical difficulties, but they did not laugh or make comments. I felt proud of Jacob and proud of my students who felt that Jacob's message was more important than his Tourette's.

Every other student had "purchased" items for personal use such as toys, videos, CDs, bicycles, and skateboards. Jacob, however, had a different idea. He wrote a report about purchasing clothing for children who had been temporarily displaced from their homes as a result of floods, fires, hurricanes, or earthquakes. He went on to explain to the class that his family certainly wasn't rich, and there were many things he thought about buying for himself or his brothers, yet he had decided to help homeless children who, because of natural disasters, had lost all their toys and personal items. Jacob hoped his contribution would help less fortunate children through a rough time. His generosity was inspiring.

As Jacob finished his oral report, many of his classmates, impressed with his unselfish act, gave him a standing ovation. Several students verbally acknowledged him for what he had done. I was so moved that during my lunch period that day, I shared the experience with other teachers; when I finished, there wasn't a dry eye in the faculty room.

That evening, I called Jacob's parents to praise his kindness. They told me they were not surprised. Apparently this young man often went out of his way to make friends with persons less fortunate than himself because of his simple and innocent desire to help others through their pain and difficulty. He just wanted to do his part to help make life a bit easier and more tolerable for others.

After the conversation with Jacob's parents, I reflected on the possibility that Jacob's experience with Tourette's syndrome had contributed to his sense of empathy and compassion for others. Regardless, I realized that it had been simultaneously both a humbling and inspiring experience knowing this unselfish ten-year-old boy. Jacob taught me—and my students—what it means to be courageous, generous, and kind.

Thank you, Jacob!

D. ROSE
El Dorado Hills, California

Long-Term Benefits

$\mathcal{N}$INE YEARS AGO, Ileah entered my multi-age classroom as a fifth grader. She was a shell—withdrawn and languid. Not surprisingly, Ileah had already developed the pattern of missing more school than she attended. She was the oldest child in her family, the first to come to our school. Each morning, Ileah had a twenty-five minute bus ride from a low-income area of our city. Often she missed the bus in the early morning hours. Her mother suffered from depression and had trouble managing the basics of life. Understandably, she was not responsive to my calls of concern or the legal truancy letters. If anything, she only felt harassed.

After lengthy discussions with other staff members, we agreed that Ileah seemed to have no inner dialogue, no reflection, and no self-direction. My first task, therefore, was to have Ileah connect to school. I showed Ileah's picture to the lunchroom people, the engineers, the educational assistants—anyone who might see her at school. I asked them to make a special effort to talk to her. "Greet her by name. Tell her you're glad to see her at school today. Ask her how she's feeling." I wanted Ileah to know others noticed her presence and cared about her.

Ileah continued to miss school. One cold winter morning she came in wearing a damp sweatshirt. She was shivering and chilled to the bone. We didn't see her again for a week. Another time she said she had no clean clothes, so she couldn't come to school. I rounded up some sweat shirts and jeans in her size and sent them home.

Over time, Ileah's mother became more comfortable with me. She didn't make excuses when I called. When I sent a taxi to pick her up for conferences, she came to school. She agreed to have the school computer dial her home each school day to help get her family up in the morning.

Over time, our interventions made a difference. Ileah began to know and be comfortable with adults around our school. If the office needed a student to help staple flyers, I sent Ileah. When the lunchroom needed help, I sent Ileah. Slowly, she began to build connections. She lifted her head a little more and occasionally smiled. She felt our care and began to feel safe. Then, little by little, she started learning. By the end of the year, I had a commitment from Ileah and her mother that next year, Ileah would be in my multi-age classroom each and every day, learning.

As a sixth grader, Ileah did much better. Trust and safety issues had been resolved. Basic human needs had been met.

She was able to focus on learning normal academic subjects. By January, Ileah seemed like a "normal" sixth grader. She had learned to ask for help when she didn't understand, and she had taken on tutoring a second grader. My heart was warmed.

I checked in with Ileah about once a month during her seventh and eighth grades at our school. The year after she graduated, her fifth-grade sister, Sabrina, joined our class. Ileah's mother had developed even more trust in me and the school. Sabrina came to school regularly and was fairly easy to teach. She had a shy smile and an irresistible twinkle in her eye. Now, I could call mom with concerns about Sabrina without mom becoming defensive. I continued to check on Ileah, who was doing fine in her new school.

Shortly after Sabrina graduated, Candace, the third daughter came into my class. Candace had more learning difficulties, but she was a hard worker. Support systems were already in place for her because our school had grown to know the family. Candace and I worked well together and she graduated from eighth grade.

The following November, our school had an open house celebrating a two-year renovation project. To my delight, Ileah, Sabrina, Candace and their mother entered my room with warm hugs and radiating smiles. It had been nine years since I first started working with Ileah. Nine years of mom growing with her three girls. Their joyful news resonated in my ears. Ileah was in her first year at Metro Community College. Sabrina was doing well in her high school. Candace missed being at our school, but was adjusting to ninth grade.

Mom had passed her high school equivalency exam and had gotten a job. They had moved into a better neighborhood. They were happy.

Children must feel safe and supported to learn well. I give special thanks to my school, which encourages long-term involvement in our students' lives—involvement that leads to long-term benefits. I also give thanks that Ileah and her family came into my life. My heart is filled. This is why I teach.

LAUNA ELLISON
Minneapolis, Minnesota

Lesson Plan at the Fountain

$\mathcal{A}$LL MORNING THE kids had been unmanageable. The Children's Center was hot and oppressive. All forty-five kids (ranging in ages from five to ten) were going nuts. The screams and noise were deafening. Jim and Wendy, my teaching partners, looked at me.

"Irv, let's get them out of here."

"And take them where?" I asked.

"To the fountain."

So, to the fountain it was. A quick bus trip, a short walk, and we were at the Villancourt Fountain in the Ferry Building Plaza across from the San Francisco Bay.

I watched the kids jump into the water, an avalanche of laughing feet kicking up wave after wave. Three or four circles of kids splashed and laughed in the hot summer sun. Thankful, I sat back and relaxed, relieved that what had started out as a terrible day was now getting better. I glanced around and took in the surroundings.

The fountain had often been described by its critics as an abortion of water and concrete; the twisted wreckage of an ancient Roman aqueduct after an atomic blast. But to kids it was a place to roll up your pants, splash, laugh, play; and now, find a dead bird.

Dammit! If it wasn't one thing it was another. There, bobbing on the waves, was a dead pigeon. Belly upward, claws curved around an invisible branch, it floated from one side of the pool to another. Wherever it drifted it brought with it uncomfortable silence.

Sasha and Erin were fastidious. They stood at the edge of the pool and glared with disgust and indignation at the bird. What right did a dead pigeon have to float in their fountain? They soon realized they needed more than their disgust and indignation to make the bird go away. They looked around for help. Wendy and Jim were nowhere to be seen. It was up to me.

Resigning myself to action, I sighed, slowly rose, and rolled up my pants. I took off my shoes, picked up an old newspaper, and stepped into the fountain. The pigeon bobbed away as I reached for it. I waded slowly and carefully toward the bird, trying to make as few waves as possible. After some time, I finally was able to maneuver myself close enough to scoop the bird up in my newspaper. My original intent was to simply pick up the bird and toss it into the nearest trash can. As I straightened up with the small body balanced on the newspaper, all human sound stopped. In the distance I could hear the autos humming on the overhead freeway. Time stood still. Forty-five pairs of silent expectant eyes hung intently on me. I glanced down at the limp body framed in soggy headlines. I looked up slowly meeting the eyes of the expectant children. It was a surreal moment. My plans to dump the bird in the trash were instantly altered.

Very gently I wrapped the newspaper around the dead bird. Maneuvering to the edge of the fountain, I stepped out onto the cement. I walked across the plaza, up a slight rise and onto the grass under the freeway. Following me was a silent procession of curious kids, Humans in Training, "HITs," as my grandmother called them.

I could feel the hard-packed earth under my feet as we marched along. Soon we found what looked like a soft spot in the turf. I reverently laid down the body of the bird.

"Will someone get something to dig with?"

Within seconds, Adria and Cheryl popped up on either side of me, each armed with a stick. Adria's blue eyes and Cheryl's brown eyes were moist. The colored ribbons in Cheryl's cornrows added a splash of happiness to the solemn occasion as she began digging. The kids took turns, eager to help. Each one dug a little and passed the sticks on. Gradually the hole got deeper. They were satisfied that they were doing the right thing, but they were curious. Questions began to fly:

"Will the bird turn to earth?"

"Will grass grow over the grave?"

"Does a bird go to heaven?"

"Will the bird come back?"

145

"If he does, will he be a person or a bird next time?"

Good questions. I answered the ones I could. The others, I acknowledged as beyond answers, as matters of each person's faith or belief. The kids looked at me nodding as if they understood.

While we talked, Jason the oldest and the biggest, asserted himself. At ten years old, Jason was as big as I was. Shoulders squared, he picked up the pigeon and carefully lay the body into the grave. I watched Adreanne, a big fan of scary stories about vampires and witches start writing on a sheet of paper. She passed the paper and pen on to another kid who scribbled his name on the paper and passed it on. When it got to me I read it.

Cursed be the knave who disturbs this grave.
May your bones turn to stones and your eyes no longer see.
The beauty of the sun and stars hovering above where my
    body be.

I signed my name and passed it on. Adreanne placed the paper in the bird's curved claws. Jason wrapped the stiff little body in the newspaper and laid it back into the grave. He picked up a handful of dirt and sprinkled it over the pigeon. Slowly he got out of the way. Each kid in turn walked up and did the same. When the last youngster stepped aside, Jason and Adreanne tried to arrange the mound to blend into the rest of the area. Overhead and all around were the sounds of cars. Tourists strolled nearby.

There we were under the freeway, forty-five little black, brown, and white kids with a grizzled old man circled around a little patch of earth saying their good-byes to a dead pigeon.

"I hope next time around it will be better," said Adria.

"I'm sorry you aren't here anymore," said Erin.

"Good luck, good bird. Farewell. Adios."

A few kids cried. We all felt sad. A living thing was no longer.

The kids began to drift back to the fountain, some in small groups, others individually. I watched them go. Soon I could hear splashing and laughing again.

Death mixed with life in a profound moment. Another day in the life of a thankful teacher.

IRV ROTHSTEIN
San Francisco, California

Special Needs,
Special Gifts

$\mathcal{N}$O TEACHER CAN ever forget that first year of teaching, and I am no exception. I was hired to teach mentally challenged students in an inner-city school. I arrived at the school at the ripe old age of twenty-two, filled with textbook knowledge yet really not knowing anything. There I began my journey.

Never has a hallway seemed longer than the one to my classroom. As I learned later, I should have been humbly grateful that it wasn't in the basement where most Special Education classes were relegated. My knees felt like jellyfish and a vise gripped my stomach and wouldn't let go. I willed myself to breathe and surmised that the curriculum, readers, math books and art supplies must be in a cupboard, but of course the existence of such materials was only a fantasy; like many Special Education teachers, I had to start from scratch.

Then came the students. These extraordinary children arrived filled with invisible gifts in hand, just for me. They came to me mentally, physically, and emotionally challenged and hence encouraged me to be the best teacher and person I could be. They challenged me to emerge from my cocoon of complacency and ignorance. They challenged me to see a new world where children don't have enough to eat, aren't loved, and experience bad things in their lives. They looked up at me with their yearning eyes and asked me to love them, and love them I did. I fed them, held them, worried about them, and taught them when they were ready, willing, and able to learn. I cried when they were abused at home and cheered when they learned to write their names. I fed them when they were hungry and finally understood what it means to nurture another human being.

> These extraordinary children arrived filled with invisible gifts in hand, just for me. They challenged me to emerge from my cocoon of complacency and ignorance.

Everything I gave those children, they gave back to me manyfold. A smile, a nod, a hand on my arm, a thank you; these were the treasured gifts they extended to me. These exceptional kids took nothing for granted; they didn't have the luxury. Their futures were so uncertain; they held no guarantees. But the children could be assured of one thing: I would be there for them each day.

They came through the door with smiles, frowns, disheveled hair, and sleepy eyes. Stories poured out. Heroic tales of midnight escapes to safety, and gallant attempts to get to school, and I knew that math and reading would have to wait. First a hug, an empathetic ear, and tears dried. Next, a hair comb, a face wash, and breakfast. These experiences were rich with gifts for me. This was not like anything I had imagined teaching to be; this wasn't just teaching, this was learning.

> *They looked up at me with their yearning eyes and asked me to love them, and love them I did. I fed them, held them, worried about them, and taught them when they were ready, willing, and able to learn.*

Reading, math, science, social studies; where does one start? No curriculum, no books, everyone at different levels; how does one begin? I looked upon the fourteen faces staring up at me waiting to be taught. Some sixth sense deep inside of me told me that these young people were going to teach me how to teach.

First, they taught me that not everyone knows their name, address, and phone number or remembers it from day to day; or that $2 + 2 = 4$ and it will tomorrow, too. I learned to be patient.

They taught me that reading isn't just decoding letters on a page, but rather wrapping oneself into the story and really learning about the world you live in. For many of the kids this meant stories about their reality, not fairy-tale worlds so unimaginable that the kids found them impossible to comprehend. I learned to be tolerant, understanding, and inventive.

They taught me that learning has to be fun. So I learned to relax and laugh at my mistakes. When there were no books, I learned to improvise and be creative.

Of course, over time, these children grew up and moved on to other schools. I, too, moved on to other schools, as teachers do. Everywhere I taught, my treasure chest grew more and more full with gifts from my special students.

Just when I thought my trunk was stuffed to overflowing, I accepted a new Special Ed position and had to find room for more treasured experiences. For the past five years I've been teaching in a high school. Some days the gifts are harder to find with teenagers. These young people often take a lot out of me, but they have also given much in return. I'm certain I'll soon need a bigger treasure chest, because I know there are many gifts of wisdom left to come.

Because they challenge me to be the best I can be, I only hope that these incredible children who have graced my life up until now, will continue to do so for many years.

JOAN SEXTON-KUSISTO
Saskatchewan, Canada

Give Me More!

*T*HE TEACHING PROFESSION recently lost one of its most dedicated members, and I lost a friend who always inspired me to give more than I thought I was ever capable of giving.

Otto Emmelhainz was my high school drama, public speaking, and English teacher during my junior and senior years. I had heard he was a difficult teacher, one who was really stingy with the A's. He gave the most homework, the hardest assignments, and the least praise of any English teacher in the high school. What I didn't know was that he would be the best teacher I would ever have.

I still remember the first assignment he gave in English class my junior year:

"Your assignment is to solve the case of the murdered priest. The only clue you have is a partially-eaten kohlrabi."

It took me an hour and a half just to find out that *kohlrabi* is a member of the turnip family and another two hours to write my story. From that day on, I was hooked. I looked forward to every class because I never knew what to expect. I learned not only because he kept things interesting, I learned because he expected me to learn. He *expected* the best from me and nothing less.

Mr. Emmelhainz made the finest contribution a teacher can make; he helped his students help themselves. He believed in them, in their ability and in their worthiness of respect.

I would imagine that sometime during the many years of his teaching career, he was given one of those lists of how to say "good job!" a hundred different ways. He never used it. I can't remember ever getting a paper back in his class on which he had written anything but, "Give me more, Nanette. You're capable of giving more than this!" Each time, I'd read the paper over and over, trying to see in myself what he saw in me. I can't begin to count the late nights, the many sheets of paper, the curses I gave this man as I struggled to revise my work, as I struggled to "give more." Sometimes it took three or four rewrites to satisfy him before he'd say, "This is more like it. B+." I'd rewrite and turn it back in. "A−." By this time, I was usually so sick of the paper that I'd put it in my folder, vowing never to look at it again.

Mr. Emmelhainz made the finest contribution a teacher can make; he helped his students help themselves. He believed in them, in their ability and in their worthiness of respect. He did more than teach facts; he inspired growth, taught his students to think, and gave each of them a part of himself. I had always known I wanted to teach, but being his student solidified my decision. Like Mr. Emmelhainz, l didn't just want to teach; I wanted to inspire and motivate.

Mr. Emmelhainz is gone. He won't be returning to his classroom again, giving out those unusual, yet challenging, assignments and pushing students beyond their limits. Everyone he taught has a part of Otto Emmelhainz within him or her. I know I do.

I was already a teacher when I learned of his death. I was saddened and needed to talk about him. I shared memories of him with my students, and they laughed when I told them about some of the assignments he gave, as well as the comments he made that pushed and wheedled the best out of me. Even though my students will never have Mr. Emmelhainz as their teacher, he is leaving his mark on them through me, as I read one more paper and write in the margin, "Give me more. You're capable of giving more."

NANETTE WAGNER
California, Kentucky

An Unexpected Tribute

$\mathcal{M}$Y SECOND YEAR as an elementary-school principal, I worked in Alex, a small rural community in central Oklahoma. Because I was new to the school, I felt it was important to get to know my students.

While in Alex, my teaching staff introduced a reading program that encouraged students to read a variety of books. I became good friends with one fifth-grade student, W.R., because we shared an interest in similar types of books.

W.R. was a great kid. The two of us would spend time together at lunch, recess, and ball games. From time to time he would talk his teacher into letting him leave class to come to my office to discuss books he'd read. He was so eager to learn that I sometimes found it difficult to stay ahead of him.

After serving as principal for two years, I decided to move from Alex to a larger district. Telling W.R. about the move was difficult for me. During my time in Alex, W.R. and I had developed a bond and respect for each other that was incredibly special. I admired him because he did his best and always gave 100 percent of himself. I think he respected me because I took the time to talk with him; he knew I was genuinely interested in his success in school and his life in general.

I found out just how much respect and admiration W.R. had for me on the day of our end-of-the-year school awards assembly. He arrived at school that morning with my first name, "Toby," shaved on the back of his head. He explained that it was his going-away present to me. I was shocked, amused, and touched by the gesture. I was even more astonished to learn that W.R's father had helped him shave his head!

If I had retired from teaching that day, or if I teach fifty more years, I think that no other experience will touch me more deeply than W.R.'s unusual, yet heart-felt, tribute to me.

Do we impact young lives? Yes, we do. Not by knowing more than anyone else about the subjects we teach, but by caring for students and demonstrating how committed we are to their success and to their futures.

TOBY SISSONS
Duncan, Oklahoma

No Matter

*H*E IS EIGHT years old and will be entering third grade soon. He reads practically as well as you or I. He has an uncanny ability to pronounce any word put in front of him. If he doesn't know how to spell something, he asks. By the time you give him help he has the word all but spelled out for you. His interests are few, yet intense. Do you ever remember writing stories about a chameleon, a diplodocus, or an archaeopteyx when you were in second grade? He will tell you that he is going to be an animal doctor when he grows up. No matter if others call him "autistic."

His favorite is the dinosaurs. His passion is drawing them. He has books about them surrounding his table, and I'll bet he can pronounce their names better than you can. He also has books on animals from "Au-stra-leee-a." "Kangaroos are mar-soo-pee-als, you know." He will show you his books and he will read them to you, but if you want him to read, be prepared to listen. He knows that the whole book is important, not just the fanciful pictures. And, by the way, don't mention anything about those Jurassic Park movies, because that's not how dinosaurs really were. His favorite is the dinosaurs. He wishes they were alive.

Make sure that you don't interrupt him when he is talking. He knows that what he has to say is important, and he must finish. "Excuse me, but I was talking." He's neither rude nor mean, just blunt and honest. He knows that what he has to say is important, and he must finish. If you look into his eyes, you will know it too. He must finish.

Oh, those big eyes. Open to things that perhaps we don't notice, or perhaps to things that we can't see. When he talks to you he goes into great detail about the subject, whether it is dinosaurs, "mar-soo-pee-als," or his video games. It isn't often, however, that he looks you in the eye. His world doesn't allow for that. He's too busy forming opinions about something else, a flower maybe, or a butterfly hatching from it's cocoon, or perhaps a book that he is reading, or one of his many detailed illustrations. But even while his eyes focus so intensely on something else, he doesn't miss a beat on what he is telling you about.

He waited a long time for me to bring my dogs to class for a visit. He asked about them everyday. I had to be sure to bring both Molly and Kola, because the stories that I told in class were about both of them. He has a dog too, you know. Her name is Holly. "Molly rhymes with Holly."

His eyes were extra big that day. They danced with excitement. He danced with excitement. Trying to contain himself he said, "I think I'm surprised! I think I'm surprised!" As the dogs ran around the classroom, jumping and wagging their tails, the other children followed in the commotion.

When it came time to take pictures, he was in all of them, always in the front, next to the dogs. Many pictures were taken that day. He knew that I had brought the dogs just for him. After all, it is "his" world.

He has an aide especially for him. She is there to help when he drifts, when he dreams about dinosaurs being alive or becoming an animal doctor, or when confusion or rage engulfs his soul. She is there to help when he closes his eyes and sways back and forth in his chair to a serenade that only he can hear. "I'm dreeeaming, I'm dreeeaming." The other children know not to touch him. They never ask why, they just know and somehow understand. His aide is there to help when he won't do any classwork and says, "I don't belong here." She is there for him when he says, "You're no good for me!" "You're fired!" She is there to love him. And she does. We all do.

Those eyes, those big brown eyes. I wonder what they see? I wonder what they can tell us? They can look right through you, you know. They can pierce your heart, they can make you laugh, and they can make you cry. They not only *can*, they *have*.

I hope he has the chance in his lifetime to learn things that will help him have a good life. I hope he finds a place where he feels he belongs. For now, he will show you his books. He will tell you all about dinosaurs and "mar-soo-pee-als." For now, he will tell you his stories and share his wonderful drawings. He knows that what he has to say is important. No matter if others call him, "autistic." No matter.

ROSALIE PETERSON
Santa Fe Springs, California

The Lyric Passage

$\mathcal{P}$ENNY ENTERED MY high school English class one fall
day about six weeks after the semester had begun. She was a
transfer to our rural area from the city about an hour away,
and her demeanor suggested that she was not happy about the
transfer, or much of anything for that matter. Tall and rather
muscular, her attire suggested she wanted to create a perception
of hardness, a tough-lady persona. The jeans, whiskey label T-
shirt, paneled leather jacket and heavy boots were all black. As
if to maintain consistency, her short cropped hair had also been
dyed a severe black and completed the image of a formidable
young woman.

I'd been told that Penny had transferred from the larger
urban high school to live with a relative in our area. I knew little of her personal life at the time but was impressed with her

bright mind, quick articulation, and the pleasure she seemed to take in American literature.

Penny was a loner. She seldom interacted with other students in class, sat by herself in the school cafeteria, and left school promptly at the final bell to go to an after-school job. She did, however, turn in high-quality work and occasionally stopped to talk after class about a point a writer had made in a story we were reading.

Penny was intrigued with Sylvia Plath and elected to do her research project on the poet. I remember having some reservations about her choice. There seemed such a heaviness in Penny's life, and it concerned me that she was so interested in a poet whose short-lived existence had ended in suicide. Naturally, I was hesitant that the romanticism of Plath's life and death might have some hold over Penny. We had several conversations as she framed her research project, and my discomfort dissipated somewhat as I observed her enthusiasm for the artistic energy and depth of Plath's poetry.

My story jumps now from those memories of Penny in my eleventh grade classroom to ten years later when, last December, I received a letter from her. I'd had no contact with Penny since she graduated and moved on to attend a nearby state university. Her letter brought about a near-spiritual experience for me.

Penny wrote that she had recently completed a master's degree in another state and had been awarded a scholarship into a doctoral program that involved a teaching assignment. About the study and especially the teaching, Penny declared, "I'm absolutely in love with it all." She recalls in the letter that at the time she was in my high school class, her mother had died. Unable to live with her father, she had moved to our area to live with an aunt. "Those years were some of the very darkest of my life," she wrote, "and I didn't like myself or believe that I would make it most days. I struggled to fit in and find an identity and meaning for myself and my life."

She recounted some specifics of the high school lessons she remembered. And then she offered this assessment of her classroom experience, lending credibility to the faith all teachers have in what we do and offering witness to the power of the shared classroom experience:

> *You spoke a language of intellect and beauty about literature, and thus about life, that reawakened a love of learning and sustained me through the worst of times. The transformative impact your class had on me planted an internal reason to endure and strive that I am still building on today. Your interest in me as a person and student demonstrated hope and compassion, which I had little of at the time. You could not fathom how much that meant to me.*

These words validate a life of teaching. Such testimony from a student who has survived the tumultuous time of adolescence and who affirms the power of the learning community sustains the teaching life. Penny's account testifies to the results of a caring learning environment in which children are encouraged to explore and are invited to look beyond the inevitable pain and loss of the human condition. It is in such an environment where students discover the fullness that awaits them there.

The realization has become clear to me: Although Penny thrived, there are many others with whom I shared a classroom who remained discouraged, disenfranchised, and for whom the good life is an external circumstance that has no relationship to their personal reality. There is, then, the imperative sense of humility, the acceptance of the great challenge, responsibility, and privilege inherent in teaching.

NELDA REYNOLDS COCKMAN
Charlotte, North Carolina

Amazing Grace

*T*HREE YEARS AGO Michael was in my class. What I remember most about him was his speech—it was nearly incomprehensible. I quickly learned to grab on to the most communicative word in his often unintelligible messages. He spoke only to me and lived in a world disconnected from his peers. It seemed as if his experience of kindergarten was a solitary one.

This prompted puzzled reactions from his classmates, who were used to interacting eagerly, like a pack of playful puppies. From their viewpoint, their conversations with Michael were consistently rebuffed. Sometimes they'd look quizzically at him and turn away; more often they'd repeat themselves progressively louder, finally yelling at him with frustrated impatience. Unresponsively, Michael would look at them, a calm expression on his face. It was difficult to watch.

Michael's productivity in kindergarten was pretty much limited to two tasks; he'd methodically cut to ribbons whatever paper he was given, then run to the play-dough center to poke holes repeatedly in the colored clay. He once briefly eyed the sand table, but then turned and ran back to the play dough, where the other children crossly reprimanded him for not sharing.

Michael seemed content with his cutting and poking, but the world of kindergarten is also filled with building, drawing, dressing up, role playing, speaking with and listening to one's peers, and developing friendships that could last a lifetime. I knew my job was to draw Michael out of his isolated world, but I wasn't sure where to begin. At that time, the testing and labels that would give him access to Special Education were years away.

Enter Gracie, who blew into town riding in her Dad's muscle car when he got a job at a nearby refinery. Like many daughters being raised by single fathers, she often wore mismatched clothes and had uncombed hair. Her footwear varied between holey sneakers and scuffed ballet slippers with shreds of glitter clinging to them. Next to her relatively well-dressed classmates, she cut quite a waif-like figure.

Because Gracie had been abandoned by her mother, she had issues with female authority. She tested the limits constantly, just to make sure I cared enough to notice. When it was story time, she would wander away from the circle, looking back until I'd have to stop reading and coax her to return. When it was time to clean up, she would continue playing, and then complain her shoes were lost, so she could stay later than the other children. She was a real heel-dragger, afraid to follow the crowd's direction for fear of disappearing from my attention.

Direct requests for compliance were often met with what I call the "trauma scuttle"—she would run away, head down, then curl up hugging her knees. Sometimes she would cry for a while. Other times, when I could afford to give special attention, I'd talk with her, hug her, reason things out. But with twenty-nine other students in the room, such opportunities came too rarely to make a lasting difference.

Each day that Gracie followed directions, the school principal rewarded her with a treat. It's an old strategy, but coupled with lots of hugs and congratulations, it works wonders for certain children. Gracie was one such child. Newly motivated, she proudly reminded me several times a day that she was doing what she was supposed to be doing. She would beam with self-approval as she walked with me to the office. It's amazing what stickers, hugs, and a little bit of attention from a woman can do for a motherless child.

While Gracie was becoming a model citizen, Michael was bearing the brunt of his classmates' misunderstanding. Time and again I heard students yelling at him: "*Michael, get in line!*" "*Michael, move!*" "*Michael, give me the clay!*" Michael continued to react without emotion. I had no way of knowing how his classmates' hostility was affecting him inside, but I knew it was driving me crazy.

One day, in response to Michael's tuneless singing, one of the bigger boys hit him. I knew it was time to have an important class discussion. In the company of another teacher, Michael made a special trip to the library while I tried my best to explain to his peers his still undiagnosed dilemma. I asked them to imagine how hard it would be if no one could understand what they were saying. "What if you were in another country and you didn't speak or understand the language? Would you want people to yell at you all day? How would that make you feel?"

"Sad," they replied in chorus.

"But even if you couldn't understand or talk to anyone, how would you feel if everyone smiled at you and used a friendly voice and shared with you?"

"Happy!"

"Michael doesn't always understand what you say to him, and you might not be able to understand what he says to you. But even if you can't understand each other, make sure you use a friendly voice. Smile at him! Share with him! Give him a hug! Michael doesn't want everyone to yell at him all day. He wants to be friends, just like you do."

Gracie sat rapt through the whole discussion. When Michael returned to the room, she demonstrated that she had taken our words of caring to heart.

Gracie went straight to Michael and began poking holes in play dough, echoing his solitary play. At first he hardly noticed her, but she kept talking to him, and pretty soon he was talking back. I have no idea what the conversation was, or if you could even call it one; I only know that Gracie was smiling, happy to be nurturing someone else whose needs seemed greater than her own at that moment.

Their play persisted, and soon they were poking holes together in the same piece of clay. Michael held a frozen grin on his face, more expression than I'd ever seen from him. Gracie hugged him, grabbed his hand, and then a little miracle happened. She pulled him away from the clay. Caught up in the moment, he forgot to run back to it. Barbie high-heels clopping, Gracie led him to the block center. Gracie poured out the blocks and began building, handing blocks to Michael, smiling and talking.

He cautiously added to her tower, and then I heard him laugh. It was a flat sound, without abandon, but it was his first in-class moment of demonstrable glee. The tower grew; other children joined in. Following Gracie's lead, they talked to Michael in voices soft with understanding. They finished that day, the first of many like it, in the animated peace of children playing without rancor. In the lives of Michael and his classmates, I knew that with the help of little Gracie, I had made a difference.

JENNIFER BEAN
Walnut Creek, California

New Insight

I WALKED INTO Jedidiah Smith Elementary School in October 1964 to face my first teaching job. The school smelled like every other school in which I had ever been. It was a combination of white paste, new paper, poster paint, erasers, and floor polish. Inhaling, this scent combined with the uneasy feeling in my stomach and suddenly I wanted to turn around, run out of there, and never return!

Jedidiah Smith was in a low-income area of San Francisco. It was in the middle of the projects, most of which were two- and three-story concrete buildings much in need of new paint. The so-called plum jobs in the district had all been taken. The only teaching positions available to novices like myself, were in the toughest neighborhoods.

I was told that my fifth-grade class had gone through three different teachers since school had started. The exhausted vice-principal, in a worn gray suit, took me upstairs. I peeked at the class through a window in the door. The kids didn't appear to be as menacing as I had expected, but they were definitely not quiet. The vice-principal told me that the current teacher was unwilling to finish out the week and asked if I could start the next day.

I arrived early the next day and was greeted by the principal who told me to get my class out of the play yard and take them upstairs. I hoped she couldn't tell that my legs were shaking. My class was easy to spot—they were making the most noise and were the only ones not lined up. I managed to put on an air of authority and lead them to the classroom in some semblance of order. To my surprise, they entered the room and actually sat down, but then the "fun" began. Staring at me, they made wise cracks using language and phrases that I'd never heard. One boy raised his hand. When I called on him, he proudly informed me that they had gotten rid of three teachers so far and that I would be next. Jeers and laughter exploded until I finally quieted them long enough to tell them that I planned to stay. Using every bit of charm, ingenuity, and gut-level trick of the trade I could think of, I survived that first day. I was young, idealistic, and determined not to give up.

In spite of their tough veneer, the kids took a liking to me. Perhaps it was due to my youth, enthusiasm, and maybe even my vulnerability. They began to respond in such as way that I could actually do some teaching. In spite of many rough spots, the next few days became somewhat easier.

DARRYL SAT BY himself. He was a brown-skinned boy with messy hair and teeth too large for his small mouth. His clothes, on any given day, were either too small or too big. I don't recall ever seeing him in a shirt, pants, or jacket that fit. He appeared to be wearing clothes taken straight from the laundry bin—every article of clothing he wore was wrinkled.

He had been placed right in front of the teacher's desk by one of my predecessors. I soon discovered why. Darryl's favorite activity was to reach out and touch or hit anyone passing his desk. He refused to participate in lessons or oral reading. His handwriting was no more than a scrawl and he never managed to stay within the lines.

As the days passed, he would grin occasionally, showing his large teeth. I was never quite sure what amused him. For the next two weeks, I tried every positive approach I could think of to get Darryl to participate. I had small successes with him in the classroom, but none on the playground. He couldn't kick the ball in a straight line during the kickball games. He couldn't hit a baseball. The cool kids shunned him and the loners ignored him in a desperate attempt to elevate their lowly status. He played alone at recess, often standing and spinning around and around. Darryl was living in his own lonely world.

I began reading *Tom Sawyer* to my class every day and they were loving it. Once I looked over at Darryl during a lesson. He had picked up the book from my desk and was trying to read it. He had the book so close that it touched his nose! It was the first time that I realized that he couldn't see. Then I remembered that the office manager had told me Darryl had not been at our school for very long. It occurred to me that perhaps he had not been at *any* school long enough for anyone to discover that he had a serious vision problem.

The very next day I arranged for the school nurse to screen him. She immediately referred him to a local optometrist who treated low-income patients. His mother didn't drive, but they could take a bus to the appointment.

Three weeks later Darryl appeared at the classroom door, proud and smiling, with his new "coke bottle" glasses. I made sure that every child in the class knew there would be hell to pay if they so much as smirked at those glasses.

When we went out for P.E. that day, Darryl played kickball and made it to first base! In class, he no longer had the need to reach out and grab other children because now he could see them. He was an avid reader, absorbing everything he could get his hands on. Sometimes he wanted to read all day and I let him! He could see well enough now to form letters correctly and write on the lines of his paper.

One day, he asked if he could take *Tom Sawyer* home to read. I gladly gave him my copy and told him to keep it. My biggest reward was the unexpected hug he gave me. He clung to me as if he'd never let go.

Thirty-five years later, I am at the end of my teaching career and preparing to retire. I will always remember Darryl's smiling face the day he got his new glasses. I have often wondered what became of him and what he is doing now. My prayer is that he is alive, well, happy, and that he is still reading.

BETTY ARNOLD
Walnut Creek, California

Beyond Street Smarts

$\mathcal{W}$HEN I FIRST met Michael, he was seven years old, with a sporadic school-attendance record. He lived with his grandmother, aunts, and numerous cousins in a small apartment. His parents were divorced, and his father lived in a neighboring city with a girlfriend. The only thing we knew about Michael's mother, was that she was in violation of probation and classified as "Whereabouts unknown." Truant officers and family members had their hands full with this young boy. When he was delivered to school, he ran away. He simply hated being there. After repeated acts of defiance and behavioral outbursts in a regular classroom, Michael was assigned to my Special Education classroom.

The first thing we all noticed about Michael was his smell. We wondered if he had ever used soap and water. He wore men's size clothing that hung about him in stiff dirty folds. His fingernails were black with grime and his hair filthy. But his smell was my biggest concern. With a room full of defiant young boys, Michael became an instant target of ridicule. It was clear that the first thing he needed was some simple physical care. With his family's lack of support, this would prove to be a daunting task.

We started with his clothes. With the help of a neighboring Wal-Mart and their charity coordinator, we obtained new clothes for Michael. We had a stack of socks, underwear, shirts, and jeans. If Michael came to class and stayed, he could choose an outfit to take home at the end of the day. It worked! The first whole week that Michael attended school, he did so in clean clothes that actually fit! Then we worked on his personal hygiene. We taught him how to scrub his hands and use a brush and clippers to clean his nails. We spoke to all the students about such issues and how to take care of themselves. We worked diligently to stop the teasing in the classroom. I found that most of my kids came from similar backgrounds, and as they got to know each other, these similarities fostered more compassion between them.

At first Michael came for the clothes, but pretty soon he was forgetting to choose new items on the way out the door. Michael had found a safe place. I believe he kept coming for the love we gave him and the learning that was starting to occur.

With the physical care issues addressed, it was time to focus on his education. Michael was big for his age and unable to read. Coupled together, these two aspects didn't exactly nourish self-esteem. I made it a point to not draw attention to his reading problem. I never demanded that he read, but encouraged him to join the circle and follow along. We sometimes worked on "echo reading," during which I would read a short sentence to Michael and he would echo it back. During group activities, we used a reading program that most of the students enjoyed. I waited patiently for Michael to display his reading readiness.

Finally, one day after weeks of patience, it happened; Michael volunteered to read in group. Inwardly I was elated, but I tried to act cool. I didn't want to scare him away from this first attempt. After Michael struggled through his first sentence he raised his eyes from the page to look at me. Unable to contain the joy I felt, my tears flowed freely as Michael beamed up at me with the first real smile I'd ever seen on his face. The breakthrough had occurred.

From that day on, we couldn't keep Michael away from school. He took a new pride in his appearance and attitude and began to find joy in learning. He'd even come to school sick, insisting he was "just fine." He wanted to learn, and, thankfully, we had found a way to help him do so. Eventually Michael grew too old to remain in my classroom.

I still see Michael occasionally at school functions and he often stops to say hello. I'm pleased that he still looks good. He sometimes demonstrates behavior and attitude problems in school, probably because he sees himself as a tough little street kid. However, now Michael is a tough little street kid who has discovered the joy of learning. He now knows he is worthy of someone's care and attention; he had only needed some encouragement, love, and guidance. Don't we all?

STACY CLARKSON
Chandler, Arizona

Care Packages

$\mathcal{L}$AST YEAR I began collecting soil samples from around the country for a class project thinking it would be fun for my students to see how soil varies from state to state. A teacher from Chattanooga, Tennessee whom I had met on the Internet, sent me several samples and said she would send more as she traveled throughout the country during the summer. We became "cyber pals" and stayed in touch. Coincidentally, we are both named Chris.

In mid-September, Chris e-mailed me with the news that there had been a devastating fire in a low-income apartment house where some of her students lived. The fire still raged out of control when the school bus dropped off the children in front of their burning homes after school that day. Several apartments were destroyed leaving eight families virtually homeless. Miraculously, no one was hurt.

I posted Chris' e-mail on a school bulletin board the next day. Our school custodian helped me set up a large table next to a poster I made requesting help for the eight unfortunate families. The response was overwhelming! Within days, our students and staff had brought personal supplies, sheets, towels, toys, games, books, laundry products, school supplies, and clothing. Enough to fill up more than twenty boxes. I e-mailed Chris who couldn't believe we had collected so much in such a short time.

Although all the supplies were boxed up, I realized I had no way to get all the stuff from Indiana to Tennessee. That evening, I racked my brain trying to figure out how to get the supplies to the families at Chris' school. The next morning, I contacted my sister-in-law who works as a dispatcher for a local trucking company. I asked if she knew any truckers who might be driving south and willing to put our load on their truck. Before noon that day, I received a call from the safety director of the trucking company. He said he would be glad to help and would pick up the donations himself and arrange to have them put on a train to Dalton, Georgia. One of his truckers would then pick up the supplies in Dalton and deliver them to Chattanooga.

I excitedly e-mailed Chris the news. She notified her principal who informed the students and their families that supplies were on the way. When the truck arrived on Monday, everyone at Chris' school was there to greet the driver. The students and staff helped unload the truck. The donations were then distributed to the appreciative families.

Within a few days, we received many wonderful thank-you notes and photos from Chris' school. I posted them on a hallway bulletin board so our school community would feel acknowledged for the difference they had made.

We have never met any of the people in Chattanooga, and probably never will. But this project has been very satisfying, nonetheless. I feel grateful to work in a school that proved itself to be so generous to total strangers. Although I know that what we sent them will never replace what they lost, it did let them know that people really do care.

When I e-mailed Chris last week and told her that our school was trying to collect one million pop tabs for the Ronald McDonald House, she responded that her school would begin collecting the tabs too, not only to help the organization, but as a way to say thank you. I guess random acts of kindness are contagious!

CHRIS SMITH
Fort Wayne, Indiana

Bad Day, Good Day

$\mathcal{M}$Y ALARM DIDN'T go off this morning. I awoke in that panic state. You know the feeling, when your body can't catch up with your mind. I was running a half hour late to school. Today was not a very good day.

I had to choose between breakfast and a shower. Hunger won. I dumped some Rice Krispies in a bowl and poured in the milk. One bite and I knew the milk was sour. Today was not a very good day.

In a rush, I was on my way, only to get held up by the world's longest freight train. While sitting idle for what seemed like hours, the gas tank "empty" light came on. Today was not a very good day.

They were refueling at the gas station; closed for a half hour. I had to go completely out of my way to find another. Today was not a very good day!

Finally I was on the highway for my hour-long morning commute. I was beginning to calm down. No sooner did I start singing with the radio, enjoying my drive, when a log truck going one way and I the other, met at a very large puddle. A muddy wave hit my small car and I couldn't see out of the windshield. I turned on my wipers but they only smeared the mud. Straining to see, I tried my washers but they were empty; I had to pull over. Today was not a very good day!

An old T-shirt and a bottle of 7-Up later and I was on my way again, but now I had to empty my bladder. I still had a half hour drive ahead of me. Today was not a very good day!

Arriving at the office, I grabbed my messages and ran to the rest room. The bus driver for my Special Ed preschool class was lost and needed an address by quarter after eight. It was now a quarter 'til nine. Today was not a very good day!

THREE-YEAR-OLD Caleb heard his parents' alarm go off in the next room. His ridged body lay still as he listened for the familiar footsteps of his mother. They exchanged smiles. "Caleb," she grinned, "You slept through the night, no seizures. Today is a very good day!"

She began the laborious morning routine that any parent of a child with cerebral palsy knows well. She laid him down on the floor and began the exercises that were difficult for Caleb. She talked and sang to him to make the time more pleasurable. "Caleb," she said, "Your legs loosened up quickly this morning. Today is a very good day!"

Like every day, she held up two shirts and asked which he wanted to wear. Only able to produce a few simple words he would usually just point. Today she asked, "Would you like the bear shirt or the airplane shirt?" Caleb said "Bear!" Today is a very good day!

She placed him in his high chair with a bowl of Rice Krispies and put the spoon in his hand as she did with every meal. She guided his stiff little arm to his mouth. The phone rang, and she left him with the spoon. It wasn't long before he had milk and Rice Krispies all over himself. When she returned she smiled and said, "Caleb, you were trying to feed yourself with the spoon. Today is a very good day!"

She propped him up with his favorite toy and went to do a few things for herself. When she returned she noticed his props had dislodged and he was sitting independently. "Caleb, you are sitting up. Today is a very good day!"

She loaded Caleb, the diaper bag, his wheelchair and his bike into her van and exclaimed "Caleb, I didn't forget anything, we are ready to go to school; today is a very good day!"

When Caleb's smile and big blue eyes rolled into my classroom that morning, it suddenly dawned on me. It wasn't such a bad day after all.

BETSY NORRIS
Eugene, Oregon

To Change a Life

I AM NOT an educator. However, at fifty years of age, I am acutely aware of how teachers have profoundly affected my life and the lives of my children. My story begins a very long time ago when I was a kid.

I had just come home from school. My parents were talking quietly; their words masked by the background sounds of TV, but I knew what the next words would be.

"Your father is being transferred, so we will be moving again," my mother said softly, hoping not to upset me. She and my father looked at each other. They were loving and support-ive and trying to diminish the impact of our latest relocation. What they didn't realize is that I wasn't upset at all. In fact I looked at it as a new chance; a time to start fresh. Maybe this time I would do well in school. Maybe this time I would make some good friends. Maybe this time things would be different.

In the past, it had always turned out the same: always the new kid on the block, off by myself, often missing assignments, getting poor grades, and day dreaming in class.

After school, however, I did what I truly loved—read books about rockets, the moon, and the stars. I read books by Willy Lay about satellites that would someday circle the globe! Wow! It was all so fascinating to me! At home I drew plans for a rocket that I fantasized about building someday. I drew them in great detail including the gyroscope, fuel pumps, combustion chamber, and so forth. That was when I was truly happy. But it was a lonely pursuit. It was the mid-1950s. Sputnik had not yet been launched and there didn't seem to be much interest in such things, or so I thought.

I remember one particular day shortly after our family had been transferred. I had just started at a new school. My teacher, Mrs. Haefmann walked passed my desk and saw one of my rocket drawings in my folder.

"What's this?" she asked.

Oh no, I'm in big trouble! I thought.

Then, to my surprise, she said, "This is amazing! Did you draw this?"

"Yes," I replied. I could feel my heart pounding with excitement and my face beaming with pride. She asked if she could put my drawing on the bulletin board to which I, of course, agreed.

After class each student looked at the drawing with intense interest and asked a lot of questions. What a special day that was. That was the day that changed my life! Mrs. Haefmann believed in me. I heard genuine excitement in her voice. Later, one of the boys introduced himself. He said he was interested in rockets, radios, and all kinds of "neat stuff," and he invited me to stop at his house after school. While at his home, we listened to his short-wave radio, and for the first time in my life I heard voices from all over the world and a million beeps, buzzes, hisses, and other curious sounds. It was all so exciting. We began to have long conversations and became very good friends.

I became diligent about my homework. Soon I began to discover the excitement of learning. My grades shot up and for the first time, I was having a great social life. School had become an adventure and I actually looked forward to going each day.

Now, forty years later, I sometimes think of Mrs. Haefmann. I wonder where she is. I wonder if she knows the effect she had on my life. I wonder how many other lives she changed.

My story now fast forwards to about seven years ago when my son, Bryan's grade-school band director suggested he audition for a community youth ensemble. He passed the audition. Several months later I went to hear their first concert. What I heard absolutely stunned me! Here was a group of about 100 grade-school and high-school students each playing with all the passion of Brahms and the discipline of marines! I closed my eyes and couldn't distinguish their artistry from a professional symphony orchestra. It was truly incredible!

As I watched and listened, I asked myself: What was the catalyst for this event? What turned these young children into seasoned artists? The answer came to me as I watched Bryan's teacher, Professor Tom Dvorak conducting. I observed his every movement from his feet to his finger tips, the wave of the baton, his body language as he crouched submissively to a pianissimo passage, and then abruptly attacked with baton to a fortissimo explosive section. I observed his rapport with them and his obvious love and respect for each student. And over the next four years I saw him give these youngsters a glimpse of greatness. I saw him teach them the meaning of commitment. I saw my son and hundreds of other students grow in their ability to focus, excel in their skills, and develop character and dignity. He gave them gifts they can never repay. I was inspired when I learned that, by day, he was a college professor. He took time out of his evenings to teach these youngsters when he could have just as easily been home relaxing. Instead, he was giving endlessly of his talents, energy, and enthusiasm.

> *Under a microscope we are all made of the same basic stuff. But from each unique combination of flesh and blood, mind and spirit, comes a unique human being, each with a special talent.*

One night Bryan and I were having a talk. I said, "That teacher must really raise a ruckus with you kids to get you to perform like that." His reply was, "No Dad, we're not afraid he might yell. It's just that we respect him a lot and we don't want to let him down."

I realized that there are only twelve notes, and from their various combinations has come everything from *Chopsticks* to *Beethoven's Ninth Symphony*. Likewise, under a microscope we are all made of the same basic stuff. But from each unique combination of flesh and blood, mind and spirit, comes a unique human being, each with a special talent. Without instruction and inspiration however, talent lies dormant.

> *The engineer may build computers, the architect may design buildings, and the chef may prepare a fine meal. But a teacher, a teacher inspires!*

The engineer may build computers, the architect may design buildings, and the chef may prepare a fine meal. But a teacher, a teacher inspires! From an idle possibility, a teacher turns talent into skill and helps mold and change an entire life.

So where are the good teachers today? If someone asked me, I'd have to say they are *everywhere*. They have been at every crossroads in my life. They have given life's greatest gifts to my son and daughter. To anyone considering a career as an educator I would ask what career could have a more positive influence on our society?

As a former student and as a parent, my advice to all teachers: Sit back every once in a while and contemplate the far-reaching effects and the importance of what you do. You have chosen a career like no other and you should be proud.

PAUL NEBEL
Muskego, Wisconsin

About the Author

ESTHER WRIGHT, M.A., worked in the San Francisco public schools for more than 20 years as a teacher and administrator. Currently a nationally recognized educational consultant, she has presented workshops for teachers throughout the United States and Canada. She lives in San Francisco, California.

Do you have a special *Why I Teach* story?
We would love to hear it.

Please send your story to:

Esther Wright
c/o Prima Publishing
P.O. Box 1260BK
Rocklin, CA 95677

Or submit your story to Prima's Web site at:

HYPERLINK http://www.primalifestyles.com/wit

PLEASE NOTE

Prima may want to publish your story and your name in a future version of this book. By submitting a story, you agree that Prima shall own all rights to the story, including the right to publish the story and use your name in a future version of this book. Prima does not pay any compensation for the use of stories submitted. Stories should not be submitted by any person under the age of 18 and should not contain any obscene or graphic or explicit sexual material or any other illegal material of any kind.